THE

LUXURY

COLLECTION®

EXTRAORDINARY
CELEBRATIONS

THE
LUXURY
COLLECTION®

EXTRAORDINARY CELEBRATIONS

ASSOULINE

CONTENTS

7   FOREWORD BY ELISE TAYLOR

11   STORY OF THE LUXURY COLLECTION

JANUARY

14   **THE SANTA MARIA**
BOQUETE FLOWER AND COFFEE FESTIVAL, PANAMA CITY, PANAMA

15   **HOTEL MARIA CRISTINA**
TAMBORRADA FESTIVAL, SAN SEBASTIÁN, SPAIN

16   **ITC WINDSOR**
FLOWER SHOW, BENGALURU, INDIA

17   **ITC GRAND CHOLA**
PONGAL, CHENNAI, INDIA

18   **SHERATON ADDIS**
TIMKET, ADDIS ABABA, ETHIOPIA

19   **THE PHOENICIAN**
FIESTA BOWL, SCOTTSDALE, ARIZONA

20   **ITC RAJPUTANA**
JAIPUR POLO, JAIPUR, INDIA

21   **HOTEL IMPERIAL**
NEW YEAR'S CONCERT, VIENNA, AUSTRIA

FEBRUARY

22   **HACIENDA PUERTA CAMPECHE**
CARNIVAL, CAMPECHE, MEXICO

24   **ITC GRAND GOA**
GOAN CARNIVAL, GOA, INDIA

25   **ITC GRAND CENTRAL**
KALA GHODA ARTS FESTIVAL, MUMBAI, INDIA

26   **THE CANYON SUITES AT THE PHOENICIAN**
ARABIAN HORSE SHOW, SCOTTSDALE, ARIZONA

28   **HOTEL GRANDE BRETAGNE**
CLEAN MONDAY, ATHENS, GREECE

30   **THE HYTHE**
VAIL LEGACY DAYS, VAIL, COLORADO

31   **ITC MUGHAL**
TAJ MAHOTSAV, AGRA, INDIA

MARCH

32   **THE ROYAL HAWAIIAN**
HONOLULU FESTIVAL, WAIKIKI, HAWAII

34   **ASSILA**
21,39 JEDDAH ARTS, JEDDAH, SAUDI ARABIA

36   **ITC KAKATIYA**
UGADI, HYDERABAD, INDIA

37   **AL MAHA**
THE DUBAI WORLD CUP, DUBAI, UAE

38   **HOTEL PARACAS**
VENDIMIA'S FESTIVAL, PARACAS, PERU

39   **NA LOTUS HOTEL**
SAN YUE SAN, NANNING, CHINA

40   **ITC MAURYA**
HOLI, NEW DELHI, INDIA

42   **REGES**
ALAÇATI HERB FESTIVAL, CESME, TURKEY

45   **THE LAGUNA RESORT & SPA**
NYEPI, BALI, INDONESIA

46   **THE NAKA ISLAND**
OPEN HOUSE DAY, PHUKET, THAILAND

APRIL

50   **EXCELSIOR HOTEL GALLIA**
SALONE DEL MOBILE, MILAN, ITALY

51   **ITC KOHENUR**
RAMADAN & EID, HYDERABAD, INDIA

52   **HOTEL ALFONSO XIII**
THE SEVILLE FAIR, SEVILLE, SPAIN

54   **SHERATON GRANDE SUKHUMVIT**
SONGKRAN, BANGKOK, THAILAND

56   **THE GWEN**
EXPO CHICAGO, CHICAGO, ILLINOIS

58   **THE WHITLEY**
ATLANTA DOGWOOD FESTIVAL, ATLANTA, GEORGIA

59   **THE ST. ANTHONY HOTEL**
SAN ANTONIO'S FIESTA, SAN ANTONIO, TEXAS

60   **VEDEMA RESORT**
HOLY FRIDAY, SANTORINI, GREECE

61   **SLS HOTEL BEVERLY HILLS**
COACHELLA, BEVERLY HILLS, CALIFORNIA

MAY

62   **PALACE HOTEL**
BAY TO BREAKERS, SAN FRANCISCO, CALIFORNIA

64   **TAMBO DEL INKA**
LORD OF TORRECHAYOC, VALLE SAGRADO, PERU

65   **HACIENDA UAYAMON**
VIRGEN DE FÁTIMA, UAYAMON, MEXICO

66   **HOTEL CALA DI VOLPE**
CAVALCATA SARDA, COSTA SMERALDA, ITALY

68   **HOTEL IVY**
DOORS OPEN MINNEAPOLIS, MINNEAPOLIS, MINNESOTA

69   **SUIRAN**
MIFUNE MATSURI, KYOTO, JAPAN

70   **MATILD PALACE**
BELVÁROSI FESTIVAL, BUDAPEST, HUNGARY

72   **HOTEL ROMAZZINO**
FESTIVAL OF SAN SIMPLICIO, COSTA SMERALDA, ITALY

74   **THE PARK TOWER KNIGHTSBRIDGE**
CHELSEA FLOWER SHOW, LONDON, ENGLAND

76   **MEIXI LAKE HOTEL**
DRAGON BOAT FESTIVAL, CHANGSHA, CHINA

78   **HOTEL AUGUSTINE**
PRAGUE SPRING, PRAGUE, CZECH REPUBLIC

79   **THE ALEXANDER**
YEREVAN WINE DAYS, YEREVAN, ARMENIA

JUNE

80   **THE WELLESLEY KNIGHTSBRIDGE**
WIMBLEDON, KNIGHTSBRIDGE, ENGLAND

81   **GRAND HOTEL RIVER PARK**
CHOREA GALA, BRATISLAVA, SLOVAKIA

83   **PALACIO DEL INKA**
INTI RAYMI, CUSCO, PERU

84   **THE JOSEPH**
CMA FEST, NASHVILLE, TENNESSEE

85   **DOMES ZEEN CHANIA**
KLIDONAS, CRETE, GREECE

86   **THE OCEAN CLUB**
CABARETE KITE FESTIVAL, COSTA NORTE, DOMINICAN REPUBLIC

87   **CASTILLO HOTEL SON VIDA**
ESTIUS SIMFÒNICS, MALLORCA, SPAIN

88   **THE LANGLEY**
THE ROYAL ASCOT, BUCKINGHAMSHIRE, ENGLAND

92	AL MANARA *JERASH FESTIVAL, SARAYA AQABA, JORDAN*	101	HOTEL CLIO *CHERRY CREEK ARTS FESTIVAL, DENVER, COLORADO*	JULY
93	HOTEL THE MITSUI KYOTO *GION MATSURI, KYOTO, JAPAN*	102	PINE CLIFFS RESORT *RIA FORMOSA FESTIVAL, ALGARVE, PORTUGAL*	
94	AJMAN SARAY *LIWA DATE FESTIVAL, AJMAN, UAE*	104	THE ROMANOS *KALAMATA DANCE FESTIVAL, COSTA NAVARINO, GREECE*	
96	PRINCE DE GALLES *LA NUIT AUX INVALIDES, PARIS, FRANCE*	105	THE JAFFA *WHITE NIGHT, TEL AVIV, ISRAEL*	
97	HÔTEL DE BERRI CHAMPS-ÉLYSÉES *BASTILLE DAY, PARIS, FRANCE*	106	THE US GRANT *COMIC-CON, SAN DIEGO, CALIFORNIA*	
98	CARESSE BODRUM *INTERNATIONAL GÜMÜŞLÜK MUSIC FESTIVAL, BODRUM, TURKEY*	107	HOTEL GOLDENER HIRSCH *SALZBURG FESTIVAL, SALZBURG, AUSTRIA*	
100	VANA BELLE *SAMUI REGATTA, KOH SAMUI, THAILAND*			
108	HOTEL PITRIZZA *TIME IN JAZZ FESTIVAL, COSTA SMERALDA, ITALY*	116	ITC MARATHA *GANESH CHATURTHI, MUMBAI, INDIA*	AUGUST
110	HACIENDA TEMOZÓN *VIRGEN DE LA ASUNCIÓN, TEMOZÓN SUR, MEXICO*	117	SOLAZ *LOS CABOS OPEN, LOS CABOS, MEXICO*	
111	SANTA MARINA *FULL-MOON CONCERT, MYKONOS, GREECE*	118	THE CASTLE HOTEL *DALIAN INTERNATIONAL BEER FESTIVAL, DALIAN, CHINA*	
112	DOMES MIRAMARE *VARKAROLA FESTIVAL, CORFU, GREECE*	120	PARKLANE *LIMASSOL WINE FESTIVAL, LIMASSOL, CYPRUS*	
114	COSME *ROUTES IN MARPISSA, PAROS, GREECE*			
122	BLUE PALACE ELOUNDA *AGIOS NIKOLAOS CLIFF DIVING, CRETE, GREECE*	132	MYSTIQUE *IFESTIA FESTIVAL, SANTORINI, GREECE*	SEPTEMBER
124	HOTEL BRISTOL *WARSAW AUTUMN FESTIVAL, WARSAW, POLAND*	133	JOSUN PALACE *CHUSEOK, SEOUL, SOUTH KOREA*	
126	ITC SONAR AND ITC ROYAL BENGAL *DURGA PUJA, KOLKATA, INDIA*	134	THE GRITTI PALACE *VENICE FILM FESTIVAL, VENICE, ITALY*	
128	THE AZURE QIANTANG *OSMANTHUS FESTIVAL, HANGZHOU, CHINA*	135	HOTEL MARQUÉS DE RISCAL *FIESTAS DE LA VENDIMIA, ELCIEGO, SPAIN*	
129	THE HONGTA HOTEL *SHANGHAI TOURISM FESTIVAL, SHANGHAI, CHINA*	137	THE NINES *FEAST PORTLAND, PORTLAND, OREGON*	
130	KING GEORGE *ART ATHINA, ATHENS, GREECE*			
140	FALISIA RESORT *BARCOLANA REGATTA, PORTOPICCOLO, ITALY*	145	PERRY LANE HOTEL *PHIL THE PARK, SAVANNAH, GEORGIA*	OCTOBER
141	HOTEL BRISTOL *VIENNALE INTERNATIONAL FILM FESTIVAL, VIENNA, AUSTRIA*	146	HACIENDA SANTA ROSA *HANAL PIXÁN, SANTA ROSA, MEXICO*	
142	THE BALLANTYNE *TASTE OF CHARLOTTE, CHARLOTTE, NORTH CAROLINA*	148	THE LIBERTY *HEAD OF THE CHARLES REGATTA, BOSTON, MASSACHUSETTS*	
143	IRAPH SUI *PAANTU, MIYAKO, JAPAN*	149	ITC GRAND BHARAT *DIWALI, NEW DELHI, INDIA*	
144	PARK TOWER *MUSEUM NIGHT, BUENOS AIRES, ARGENTINA*	150	NORTH ISLAND *CREOLE FESTIVAL, SEYCHELLES*	
151	LUGAL *ANKARA INTERNATIONAL FILM FESTIVAL, ANKARA, TURKEY*	154	THE ATHENEE HOTEL *LOY KRATHONG, BANGKOK, THAILAND*	NOVEMBER
152	AL WATHBA *SHEIKH ZAYED HERITAGE FESTIVAL, ABU DHABI, UAE*	156	LAS ALCOBAS *DÍA DE LOS MUERTOS, MEXICO CITY, MEXICO*	
153	ITC GARDENIA *RAJYOTSAVA, BENGALURU, INDIA*	158	THE PRINCE GALLERY TOKYO KIOICHO *TOKYO HERITAGE WEEK, TOKYO, JAPAN*	
160	THE TASMAN *ROLEX SYDNEY HOBART YACHT RACE, HOBART, AUSTRALIA*	168	GROSVENOR HOUSE *UAE NATIONAL DAY, DUBAI, UAE*	DECEMBER
162	SANCTUARY CAP CANA *BOAT PARADE, PUNTA CANA, DOMINICAN REPUBLIC*	169	HOTEL PRESIDENT WILSON *FÊTE DE L'ESCALADE, GENEVA, SWITZERLAND*	
164	AL MESSILA *QATAR NATIONAL DAY, DOHA, QATAR*	170	HACIENDA SAN JOSE *FERIA DE REYES, SAN JOSE, MEXICO*	
166	SANTO MAURO *NAVIDAD, MADRID, SPAIN*			

ELISE TAYLOR
SENIOR LIVING WRITER,
VOGUE

Every May, Queen Elizabeth II of England put on a pastel suit and a pair of pearls to peruse the flora-filled pavilions of the RHS Chelsea Flower Show. One year, she marveled over the lady slipper orchid, a canary-yellow bloom so rare it required its own security guards. In 2019, she visited the display designed by her granddaughter-in-law the Duchess of Cambridge. (Moments before the monarch arrived, the duchess noticed a stray branch in her garden and swiftly stuffed it into her handbag. *Crisis averted.*) Another year, the queen even examined a floral sculpture crafted in her image, to mark her ninetieth birthday. Yet, despite the changing exhibits over the years, one thing always stayed the same: her genuine smile.

The Chelsea Flower Show, first held in 1862, is not the biggest horticultural festival. Nor is it the most visited. Yet it is arguably the most beloved—by the queen of England and the 157,000 other visitors who flock from all over the world to its well-manicured lawns. Why? To attend the Chelsea Flower Show is to immerse yourself in an ambience of Anglophilia, where you can stroll acres upon acres of English gardens and then enjoy a traditional afternoon tea with coronation chicken finger sandwiches as well as warm scones with jam and clotted cream. It is to both experience the London that has been romanticized for most of us since birth by Virginia Woolf, Jane Austen, Charles Dickens, and have it live up to your own great expectations.

Across the world, there are certain fairs, sporting events and celebrations that allow travelers to sense the soul of the city they are in. Salone del Mobile, the world's preeminent furniture fair, is inseparable from Milan (Hotel Excelsior Gallia, in the Porta Nuova neighborhood, pays homage to its city's design DNA by adorning its lobby with pieces from prominent firms, including B&B Italia, Cassina, Fendi Casa and Flos). The Dubai World Cup, a Thoroughbred horse race with a $12 million purse held at the spaceship-esque Meydan Grandstand, is a symbol of the Middle Eastern city's futuristic opulence.

Enthusiastic dancers performing at a festival in Brazil.

Some events are not content with just *showing* a city's culture. They want to share it, and wildly so. In January, equestrian enthusiasts—young and old, visitors and locals alike—are delighted by bouts of sportsmanship at the Jaipur Polo tournament, taking place near ITC Rajputana. Come fall, the tiny island archipelago nation of the Seychelles honors its diverse Afro-European heritage with Creole Festival. Steps from North Island, street carts serve up everything from coconut curry to fish smothered in papaya chutney, and traditional music fills the air. The weeklong celebration culminates in Bal Asosye, an all-night ball where joyful revelers can dance until seven in the morning. Meanwhile on June 24, to celebrate the winter solstice in the Southern Hemisphere, a costumed procession re-enacts the ancient Inca festival of Inti Raymi in Peru. Imperial descendants playing pan flutes and beating drums march from Koricancha— a temple across from Palacio del Inka—to Sacsayhuamán as thousands watch from balconies, cafés and grandstands.

And then there are the intimate celebrations that take place in private, rather than public, spheres. A reservation at one of Venice's most storied cafés, where convivial conversation (and red wine) flows long after the bill arrives. A private tasting room filled with your closest friends at a family-owned bourbon distillery in Savannah, Georgia. A milestone birthday spent in Bali, where the concierge plans a surprise beachside bonfire for the special occasion.

People travel for many reasons. Some seek adventure, others relaxation. Yet for those who prize culture above all, journeying to a place amid a party is perhaps the best way to immerse yourself in its values, its identity, its *joy*. After all, historian John Huizinga once said: "If we are to preserve culture, we must continue to create it."

Women dancing with baskets of flowers through the streets of Mexico.

STORY OF
THE LUXURY COLLECTION

The Luxury Collection is an ensemble of more than one hundred of the world's finest hotels and resorts, each noteworthy for its architecture, furniture, amenities, cuisine, art and distinctive heritage. Our properties all share the common goal of offering our guests authentic experiences that are inextricably linked to each destination, broadening the mind and transforming the individual. The properties are deeply connected to their local culture in ways that are rare, captivating and indigenous.

Within a world of hotels spanning five continents and countless cultural influences, The Luxury Collection celebrates the spirit of self-discovery. In this volume, we explore individual celebrations around the world that draw upon the authentic allure of our properties and their destinations. With this book as a guide, visitors can travel the world and become immersed in the local culture every month of the year. Start the new year at Hotel Imperial in Vienna and take in a moving performance by the Vienna Philharmonic. Then travel to The Gwen in Chicago, Illinois, to enjoy contemporary and modern art at the EXPO Chicago. Book accommodation at Matild Palace to kick off the summer season and experience Budapest's Belvárosi music festival. Next on the itinerary is HOTEL THE MITSUI KYOTO, where guests can attend the Gion Matsuri festival. Complete this global journey at Grosvenor House in Dubai, where guests can feel the country's pride during UAE National Day celebrations.

From the showmanship of the CMA music festival in Nashville to the vibrancy of Holi in New Delhi, our properties have selected celebrations that showcase each of their spectacular locations, inspiring a passion for travel and an appreciation for the destination around them.

JANUARY
FEBRUARY
MARCH

FLOWERS & COFFEE

In western Panama, the landscape and climate of the Chiriqui Highlands are ideal for coffee production. Courtesy of the fertile volcanic soil, visitors will find some of the most valuable coffee in the world, and a plethora of vibrant flowers. To commemorate the region's agricultural importance, the Boquete Flower and Coffee Festival takes place each **January**. When traveling to this festival, visitors would be remiss to not stop by Panama City for a stay at **the Santa Maria**.

Flower arrangements become works of art in Panama during the Boquete Flower and Coffee Festival

MARCH TO THE BEAT

The Tamborrada Festival in San Sebastián, Spain, is many things (fun, lively), but it's definitely not quiet: In this festival, which takes place on **January** 20 every year, over a hundred groups (called Tamborrada) participate in twenty-four hours of nonstop drumming. This festival started in 1836 and is meant to celebrate the city's namesake and patron saint, Saint Sebastian. The groups dress in costumes that resemble old military uniforms and play the "March of San Sebastián" throughout the twenty-four hours. **Hotel Maria Cristina** joins in on the fun by passing out drums and offering guests an exclusive dinner on the night of the festival. A Tamborrada group passes by the hotel and treats the guests to a small demonstration. Throughout the week, special themed cocktails and pastries are served to help immerse visitors in the festival.

HOTEL MARIA CRISTINA
SAN SEBASTIÁN, SPAIN

A FLORAL FANTASY

Bengaluru's 240-acre Lalbagh Gardens hosts two Flower Shows every year, one in **January,** coinciding with India's Republic Day on January 26, and the other around Independence Day, on August 15. Millions of flowers are used to create installations and massive structures, including whole flower-covered pavilions. The Flower Show began in 1912, and each show lasts about two weeks. In the artistic spirit of the show, guests at **ITC Windsor** can enjoy the curated exhibits at the hotel's WelcomArt Gallery, a space for renowned and aspiring artists to showcase their creations.

ITC WINDSOR

BENGALURU, INDIA

HARVEST TIME

Pongal is a harvest festival, so it's appropriate that it shares its name with a type of food–specifically, a special rice dish. *Pongal* (the food) features the new rice from the harvest, which is boiled with milk and jaggery (a type of unrefined sugar) and topped with cashews as garnish. Pongal (the festival) has four separate days, each with set activities, such as the bull-taming sport Jallikattu, meant to celebrate different aspects of the harvest. Of course, plenty of *pongal* is served and eaten. The festival takes place at the start of the Thai month in the Tamil calendar, typically **mid-January.** In Chennai, India, **ITC Grand Chola** offers guests a special Pongal brunch with a selection of traditional dishes. The hotel is also decorated in typical Tamil style, with flowers and vibrant floor designs to highlight the tradition and culture.

ITC GRAND CHOLA

CHENNAI, INDIA

A bull decorated for Jallikattu in the Pongal festival

TIMKET

One of the biggest and most anticipated Orthodox Christian events on the Ethiopian calendar, Timket takes place on **January** 19. The festival is meant to celebrate the baptism of Christ, and there is a specific schedule of events. On the first day, priests carry richly decorated *tabots,* replicas of the tablets of the Ten Commandments, to a body of water. The following day, people wear white clothing and headscarves, attend mass and participate in a type of ritual baptism. After that, there is a feast. The country's capital, Addis Ababa, is a great place to experience this celebration, and the **Sheraton Addis** is more than happy to accommodate festivalgoers.

TOUCHDOWN!

An all-American classic, the Fiesta Bowl is an American college football bowl game that occurs annually in late **December** or early **January** in the Phoenix area. It is one of the six major post-season games (known as the College Football Playoff New Year's Six) that host a semifinal contest on a rotating basis. The Fiesta Bowl is a nonprofit organization, providing support to deserving causes statewide through Fiesta Bowl Charities. Visitors are invited to watch the Fiesta Bowl Parade, which features bands, floats, balloons and performers. While staying at **The Phoenician** resort, guests are immersed in the college football experience during the week of the game, as the property has hosted numerous Fiesta Bowl–related events over the years and contributes to the Fiesta Bowl Charities' year-round efforts.

THE PHOENICIAN

SCOTTSDALE, ARIZONA, UNITED STATES

JAIPUR POLO

The royals of Jaipur have been avid polo lovers for generations, and the polo season swings into action in the Pink City every **January.** Players and fans arrive from across India and around the world to participate in and watch matches and tournaments–with all the attendant parties and soirees, of course. The city has played a major role in keeping polo alive and attracts new players for this sport of kings. **ITC Rajputana** has been the official hotel for the Asia Cup for the last two years.

NEW YEAR'S CONCERT

To ring in the New Year, the Vienna Philharmonic performs a New Year's Concert on **January** 1 in the Golden Hall of the Musikverein in Vienna. This prestigious event is broadcast in over ninety countries, sharing the lively yet nostalgic music from the vast repertoire of the family of Johann Strauss and its contemporaries. The historic Composers Entrance, which connects **Hotel Imperial** to the neighboring Musikverein, provides guests with a stately experience while en route to the New Year's Concert.

HOTEL IMPERIAL

VIENNA, AUSTRIA

CARNIVAL!

The oldest Carnival celebration in Mexico dates to
1582 in Campeche. Normally starting in **February**
(it takes place the week before the beginning
of Lent), the weeklong Carnival merges aspects
of Mayan, Spanish and Latin American cultures
into one very fun party. One must-see event: the
bad-mood burial, in which a doll dressed as a pirate
is paraded along the waterfront, placed in a coffin
and burned—only good moods allowed after that.
Hacienda Puerta Campeche is the ideal home
base to experience this one-of-a-kind celebration.

GOAN CARNIVAL

The Goan Carnival features the largest parade in India, as it is hosted in four cities: Panaji, Margao, Vasco and Mapusa. This popular festival usually begins on the Saturday before the start of Lent and concludes on the following Tuesday, in **February.** These parades feature dancers, musicians, fire eaters, jesters, acrobats and brass bands. Presiding over it all is King Momo, a local chosen to be the traditional leader of the festivities, who rides along on a splendid float. Streets are decorated with banners, bunting and flowers, while the evenings are given over to parties. This is also a huge food festival before many local Catholics begin forty days of austerity, as Lent begins when Carnival concludes. **ITC Grand Goa's** concierge is on hand to create special tours for guests to witness the festivities within the four cities.

An intricate bird float at one of the parades during the Goan Carnival

ART FESTIVAL

One of India's biggest art and culture celebrations, the Kala Ghoda Arts Festival lights up south Mumbai each **February.** The event brings art, food, music, dance and even stand-up comedy to audiences–there is something for everyone, including children. The events are characterized by that indescribable energy that permeates Mumbai. The concierge at **ITC Grand Central** is available to curate bespoke trips for guests to the various activities.

ITC GRAND CENTRAL

MUMBAI, INDIA

Osteen Schatzberg 2019

GIDDYUP

Since 1955, the Arabian Horse Show has been a **February** tradition in Scottsdale, Arizona, attracting a global crowd of horse owners, trainers and breeders. It is the largest Arabian-horse show in the world, with nearly 2,400 horses participating. More than just competitions, the show also features gala parties, seminars and over three hundred vendor booths. **The Canyon Suites at The Phoenician** is the preferred accommodation for attendees due to its perfect location and elegant style.

Scenes from the Arabian Horse Show and The Canyon Suites in Scottsdale, Arizona

CLEAN MONDAY

Considered one of the most important feasts in Greece, Clean Monday, occuring before the forty-day period of Lent and marking the beginning of Easter preparations, normally takes place in **February** or **March.** Orthodox Christians observe this day with a meal consisting of *lagana*, or unleavened bread, accompanied by *taramasalata* (salted and cured fish roe) and every kind of seafood, plenty of olives and *fasolada* (Greek bean soup). To complete the feast, there is scrumptious halvah for dessert. In the Greek capital of Athens, home to **Hotel Grande Bretagne,** locals and visitors gather in Philopappou, next to the Acropolis, to watch the sky fill with kites or to participate in a "climbing race," releasing the string of their kites so that they ascend as high as possible.

Hotel Grande Bretagne offers
guests a veritable feast during
the celebration

VAIL
LEGACY DAYS

Each **February,** people in Vail, Colorado, honor the legacy of the 10th Mountain Division, a rugged group of soldiers who trained to fight on skis and served admirably in World War II. During Vail Legacy Days, skiers dress in historic ski-trooper uniforms and ski down Vail Mountain by torchlight. The celebration continues with a parade through Vail Village and finishes with fireworks. **The Hythe** exists only because the people who established the Vail Mountain ski slopes served in the 10th Mountain Division during World War II. Their postwar shared vision created an iconic ski resort that attracts visitors from around the world. Vail Legacy Days immerses guests in the town's rich history.

The Hythe's restaurant, Margie's Haas, honors Colorado local Margie Haas, who opened her home to soldiers from the 10th Mountain Division and provided them with home-cooked meals

THE HYTHE

VAIL, COLORADO, UNITED STATES

WALK THE TAJ

As a self-proclaimed carnival of culture, Agra's Taj Mahotsav brings together over four hundred craftspeople and artisans who offer handmade creations representing diverse regional cultures. The festival is celebrated in **February** at the Shilpgram arts village near the eastern gates of the Taj Mahal. To ensure guests make the most of their experience, **ITC Mughal** offers a special experience called Walk the Taj, in which the ITC team helps guests explore the Taj Mahal and revel in the Taj Mahotsav. It's like having a local, savvy friend as a guide. Traditional food is enjoyed as well.

HAPPENING IN HONOLULU

Hawaii's premier cultural event, the Honolulu Festival, takes place in **March,** and it's intended to promote harmony between all the people of Hawaii and the Pacific Rim. The festival does so with a wide range of activities, including dance performances, art demonstrations and a parade. These all showcase the blend of Asian, Pacific and Hawaiian cultures that makes this part of the world so vibrant and unique. The finale of the festival is the Nagaoka Fireworks over Waikiki Beach, where guests staying at **The Royal Hawaiian** can watch the fireworks light up the night sky.

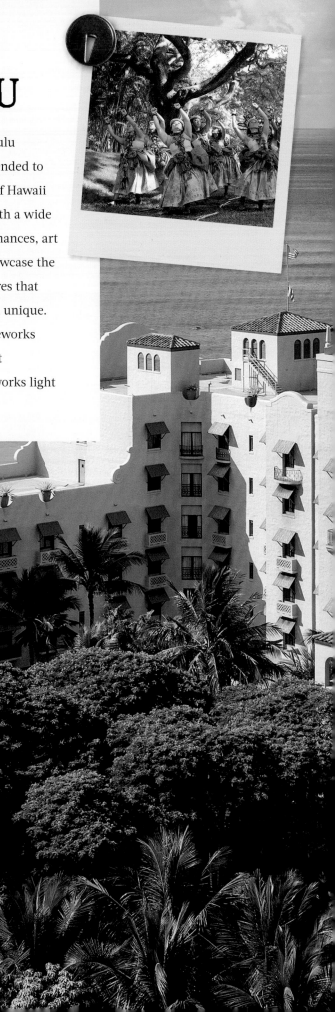

THE ROYAL HAWAIIAN

WAIKIKI, HAWAII, UNITED STATES

21,39 JEDDAH ARTS

Normally held in **March,** the festival 21,39 Jeddah Arts features exhibitions–with works by artists such as Nojoud Alsudairi, Obadah Aljefri and Manal Al Dowayan–workshops and a speaker series, focusing on the ability of art to bridge language, traditions and borders. The festival shares its name with the nonprofit initiative that hosts it, organized by the SAC. The goal of the organization is to promote and develop Jeddah's status as the vanguard in Saudi Arabia's contemporary art scene. The festival's name comes from the geographic coordinates of the city (21.54°N, 39.17°E). A gallery itself, with a collection of two thousand pieces of art, **Assila** highly recommends this event to all art and culture enthusiasts.

ASSILA

JEDDAH, SAUDI ARABIA

UGADI

A celebration of the Hindu New Year, Ugadi normally falls in **March** or April. People typically celebrate with visits to temples and charitable acts, and by decorating their homes with strings of mango leaves and *muggulu*, ornate patterns traced with colored powder. Of course, there's food: Families get together to enjoy a feast, which will always include a sort of pickle called *pachadi*. This dish combines all different types of flavors (sweet, salty, sour, bitter and spicy) to symbolize that life is a range of diverse experiences–and one must be ready to face them all in the coming year. Hyderabad's **ITC Kakatiya** celebrates this day by offering guests a traditional meal at its specialty South Indian restaurant, Dakshin. The hotel's concierge can direct guests wanting to explore the area to the best-known temples.

ITC KAKATIYA

HYDERABAD, INDIA

Mango leaves hung outside homes in India for the celebration of Ugadi

EQUESTRIAN EXTRAVAGANZA

Horse racing is an integral part of the culture of the Arabian peninsula, and is essential to the tourism industry in Dubai. The Dubai World Cup, held on the last Saturday of **March,** is the most popular race of them all, attracting visitors from all over the country and the world. **Al Maha** offers guests an exclusive equestrian experience, providing a sneak peek into the daily routine of these majestic creatures. Also, the staff at Al Maha can arrange transport to the World Cup for guests who want to experience this spectacular event. Guests are also invited to get an early look by attending the dress rehearsal, scheduled for the first Saturday of March, which allows trainers to give their horses one last pre-Cup run. At the main event, the atmosphere is lively as everyone cheers for their favorites.

VENDIMIA'S FESTIVAL

The Grape Harvest Festival of Ica celebrates the fruit that is the source of this region's delicious wines and pisco, a distilled liquor. Held during the first days of **March,** the festival celebrates the Peruvian way of winemaking, with wine tasting and tours along the local vineyards. Street parades, vibrant music and local dishes also add life to this festival. Although **Hotel Paracas** is located two hours north from the festival, the staff are happy to help guests who are traveling to the participating wineries.

HOTEL PARACAS

PARACAS, PERU

SAN YUE SAN

San Yue San, a folk-song festival, is one of the most important celebrations for the Zhuang people in Guangxi, in southern China, where **Na Lotus Hotel** is located. On the third day of the third month of the lunar calendar, which falls during **March** or April, locals don bright costumes and participate in the festivities by singing, dancing and playing traditional games. The main event, however, is the Singing Fair, where people gather to pray for good weather and a bountiful harvest. During the performances, girls toss embroidered balls to express their admiration for those they think sing well. The intricate bamboo pole dancing–a type of game in which people jump between interwoven bamboo poles–is a must-see, and visitors can even participate.

ITC MAURYA

NEW DELHI, INDIA

FESTIVAL OF COLORS

Known as the Festival of Colors, Holi generally takes place in **March,** though it's subject to change every year because it depends on the lunar calendar. On the first day of this two-day festival, people light bonfires to signify the burning of all evil. On the second day, Holi lives up to its nickname, as people throw colorful water and powders all over as a joyful celebration of life. Throughout the festival, people savor traditional food and drinks. The team at **ITC Maurya** are happy to assist guests in planning the most authentic and enjoyable Holi experience in India.

ALAÇATI HERB FESTIVAL

The Alaçatı Herb Festival, which has been organized since 2010, allows visitors to experience the unique tastes and smells of Turkey. Specialties such as mastic pudding, chewing-gum cookies and *çağla* salad rely on Aegean herbs and local flavors. Taking place in **March** or **April**, the festival showcases the windmills in Alaçatı, a symbol of the region. After a day of igniting your senses, return to the nearby, serene oasis of **Reges** in Çesme to unwind by the water and perhaps indulge yourself once more with a meal at one of the hotel's extraordinary restaurants.

ELORA HARDY

Designer and founder of Ibuku

Q: What is a celebration you can't miss each year?

The Ngerupuk processions take place the night before each Balinese Lunar New Year. Huge sculptures of demons and monsters, handmade by the young people in each village, are paraded through the streets at dusk. The purpose is to satisfy the evil spirits so the new year can begin fresh and clear. The following day no planes fly, no cars drive, everyone stays at home with lights off to rest. An atmosphere of complete peace and calm embraces Bali.

Q: Is there a unique tradition that you've experienced at a local celebration?

Segments of fresh bamboo poles are used as noisemakers. By lighting a fire in one end, they cause the internodes to break with a loud bang!

Q: How do you celebrate personal moments of joy?

A special meal cooked together with family is a simple way we love to savor a special day.

Q: What are everyday moments that you think people should celebrate more?

Being a parent to little kids makes me feel nostalgia in advance for the everyday moments. Sometimes I manage to resist that urge to rush toward the next thing, and pause at a stoplight to angle the rearview mirror so I can watch the wonder on their little faces looking out at the sky.

DAY OF SILENCE

Nyepi is the Balinese "Day of Silence," and is commemorated every Isakawarsa (Saka New Year), which generally falls in **March.** It is a day of fasting, meditation and self-reflection that starts at six in the morning and lasts a full twenty-four hours. On Nyepi Day, the Balinese have four rules that ensure there are no interruptions: no electricity, no working, no traveling and no entertainment. With no distractions, observers can revel in the starry night. During this time, **The Laguna Resort & Spa** hotel follows these rules and encourages guests to bask in the beauty of the night sky. The Laguna also urges guests, the day before Nyepi, to take in the Ogoh-Ogoh parade. Ogoh-Ogoh are giant dolls used to portray evil spirits, as the Balinese people parade the streets with loud instruments and bamboo torches. At the end, the Ogoh-Ogoh are destroyed, banishing these evil forces as people start the new year.

OPEN HOUSE

On the Naka Island off the coast of Phuket, Thailand, the Bann Koh Naka School organizes an Open House Day every **March** to celebrate the community and foster a sense of unity. This occurs right after the students' final exams, to celebrate their progress during the year. It's a fun event for locals and tourists: Koh Naka villagers and students decorate the town, and local cooks sell delicacies to snack on. **The Naka Island Resort & Spa** hotel helps by selling tickets in advance of the event and supplies pastries the day of. Guests are invited to participate and may even enjoy a performance from the ambassadors of the hotel.

THE NAKA ISLAND

PHUKET, THAILAND

APRIL

MAY

JUNE

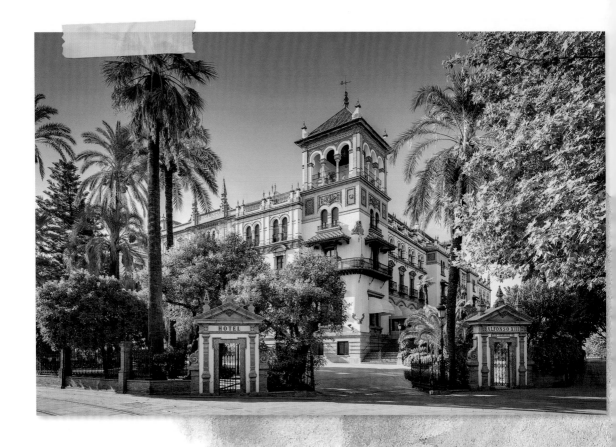

A SPRINGTIME SPECTACLE

The Seville Fair, also known as the Feria de Abril, is held annually in the Andalusian capital. It's generally in **April,** but sometimes Feria de Abril can be a bit of a misnomer, as it falls two weeks after Easter, which can be earlier or later. The fair officially lasts for six days. During the day, there are bullfights and parades, while at night there is eating, drinking and dancing. For the duration of the fair, the common areas of the **Hotel Alfonso XIII** are decked out, and the luxury cars that typically chauffeur guests are replaced with richly decorated carriages.

EXCELSIOR HOTEL GALLIA

MILAN, ITALY

SALONE DEL MOBILE

Ever since its launch in 1961, the Salone del Mobile has been the place for design lovers to come and appreciate the most innovative Italian furniture and accessories. And the Salone is just one part of a wider event. Every **April,** as part of the Week of Design, or the Fuorisalone, the city becomes the "capital of design," with events taking place all around, particularly in the iconic quarters of Brera and Tortona. Numerous exhibition spaces showcase the most cutting-edge ideas in design. The **Excelsior Hotel Gallia** participates in the fun: The hotel's façade, lobby and lounge are filled with artistic installations, offering guests the opportunity to get inspired before they even leave the building.

RAMADAN & EID

During the ninth month in the Islamic calendar, Muslims observe Ramadan, a monthlong fast from dawn to sunset. The timing according to the Gregorian calendar changes every year, but in 2023 and 2024 it will occur in March and **April.** Charity is an important element of Ramadan, and families gather ritually for *sehri*, a meal at dawn, and then *iftar*, the meal with which the daily fast is broken. The second meal celebrates the region's gastronomic riches, and the region's famous hospitality is in full display, as everyone is welcome to enjoy the food. Dishes like *haleem* (a type of meat stew), biryani (a richly spiced rice dish) and kebabs are enjoyed during the meals. The month of Ramadan comes to a close with a joyous celebration of Eid, when gifts are exchanged and a feast prepared and consumed. **ITC Kohenur** joins the spirit of Eid with special menus at the Golconda Pavilion restaurant.

ITC KOHENUR

HYDERABAD, INDIA

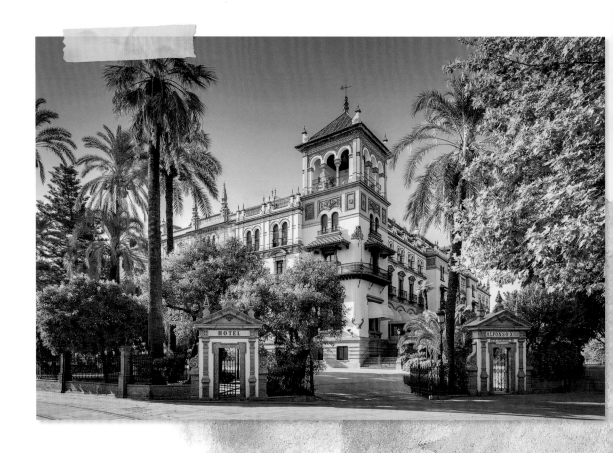

A SPRINGTIME SPECTACLE

The Seville Fair, also known as the Feria de Abril, is held annually in the Andalusian capital. It's generally in **April,** but sometimes Feria de Abril can be a bit of a misnomer, as it falls two weeks after Easter, which can be earlier or later. The fair officially lasts for six days. During the day, there are bullfights and parades, while at night there is eating, drinking and dancing. For the duration of the fair, the common areas of the **Hotel Alfonso XIII** are decked out, and the luxury cars that typically chauffeur guests are replaced with richly decorated carriages.

HOTEL ALFONSO XIII

SEVILLE, SPAIN

Traditional costumes for
the sevillana dance

SONGKRAN

A highlight of the annual cultural calendar in Thailand is Songkran, the Thai New Year–a water festival that takes place over several days in **April.** Devout Buddhists visit temples in the morning and pour water on Buddha statues, to symbolize purification. This tradition has evolved over the years to include lively water fights in the streets from dawn until dusk. At **Sheraton Grande Sukhumvit,** guests can take part in the ritual bathing of a Buddha statue and begin the Thai New Year with a blessing.

SHERATON GRANDE SUKHUMVIT

BANGKOK, THAILAND

THE GWEN

G

CHICAGO, ILLINOIS, UNITED STATES

EXPO CHICAGO

Held at the Navy Pier each **April,** Expo Chicago, a renowned
contemporary and modern art exhibition, brings together about 140
galleries from the United States and around the world to showcase
exciting works of art. Visitors can check out sections devoted to
newer galleries and books as well as legacy galleries and artists.
Blocks away from the Expo lies **The Gwen.** Housed in the landmark
McGraw-Hill building, it boasts a façade featuring bas-relief
sculptures by Gwen Lux, a pioneering female sculptor in the 1920s
and the hotel's namesake, making it an ideal–and beautiful–home
base for any art aficionado.

ATLANTA DOGWOOD FESTIVAL

The flowering dogwood tree is native to the eastern U.S. and can be found growing throughout Georgia. In Atlanta, where the tree is especially beloved, the Atlanta Dogwood Festival has been held each **April** in Piedmont Park since 1936. Today, the event attracts more than 200,000 visitors for three days of live entertainment, family activities and fine art. Like Walter Rich, the event's founder, **The Whitley** has a great deal of affection for the dogwood. The hotel includes the tree's blossom in its logo: a symbol of springtime rebirth, which parallels the rebirth of an iconic Atlanta hotel.

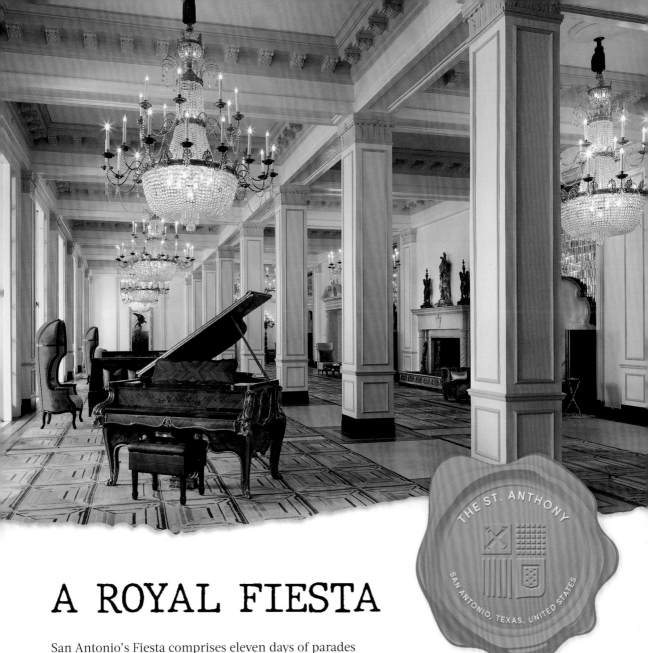

A ROYAL FIESTA

San Antonio's Fiesta comprises eleven days of parades and festive events in **April**, celebrating the city's vibrant culture as well as the heroes from the Battle of the Alamo. **The St. Anthony** hotel has hosted Fiesta royalty and many Fiesta events since the 1920s. Aside from its lavish accommodations, the St. Anthony is right in the heart of Fiesta celebrations; its location in historic downtown puts it within walking distance of the Alamo, River Walk and numerous Fiesta-event venues.

HOLY FRIDAY

Falling on the Friday before Easter, usually in **April** or **May,** Holy Friday is an imporant religious holiday in the village of Pyrgos on the island of Santorini. Located on a hill, Pyrgos is decorated with hundreds of candles and lanterns lining every walkway and trail. The light is visible across the island, creating a magical atmosphere. Guests of the **Vedema Resort** are encouraged to take part in the traditional procession of the epitaph–a truly local, one-of-a-kind experience.

VEDEMA RESORT

SANTORINI, GREECE

LUXURY ESCAPE FOR FESTIVALGOERS

The Coachella Valley Music and Arts Festival in California, with a range of acts from up-and-coming performers to all-star artists, runs over back-to-back weekends in **April.** In addition to music, the festival is known for its over-the-top art installations. Prior to making their way into the desert area where the festival is held, many attendees stop in Los Angeles to stock up on festival attire from the trendy boutiques on Melrose Avenue–conveniently, just a few minutes away from the **SLS Hotel Beverly Hills,** and guests can arrive at the shops in style via the hotel's complimentary house car. Post-Coachella, guests can enjoy the pampering services of Ciel Spa at the hotel, including restorative IV treatments and CBD-infused massages. As the festival spans two weekends, many performers choose to return to Los Angeles between sets. Guests of the SLS often encounter their favorite singers, bands and DJs riding alongside them in the elevators.

SLS HOTEL

BEVERLY HILLS, CALIFORNIA, UNITED STATES

THE
PALACE

PALACE HOTEL
SAN FRANCISCO, CALIFORNIA, UNITED STATES

BAY TO BREAKERS

Since 1912, over 2 million costumed runners and walkers have completed the iconic 12K journey through the city–from San Francisco Bay to the breakers on Ocean Beach. Bay to Breakers, the longest consecutively run footrace in the world, is built by the community and takes place each **May.** The team at the **Palace Hotel** has participated in the race on several occasions, and its expertly trained concierges have been invaluable in sourcing last-minute items for guests and participants' creative costumes. Post-race celebrations frequently occur at the hotel's Pied Piper bar and in The Garden Court.

SEÑOR DE TORRECHAYOC

The Lord of Torrechayoc festival dates from the 1860s, when a huge cross was placed in the mountainous area between the Peruvian cities of Urubamba and Lares. The Lord of Torrechayoc refers to this cross, which has become the patron saint of the region. Taking place in **May** or June, the celebration includes a religious service followed by a procession with the bejeweled cross all around Urubamba. Guests at **Tambo del Inka** can enjoy the festivities from the comfort of their hotel, as the parade runs through the main entrance. To add to the fun, there are fireworks, dancers and bullfights.

VIRGEN DE FÁTIMA

At midnight on **May** 12 of every year, guests of **Hacienda Uayamon** can hear the local community sing "Las Mañanitas," a folk song that is typically sung on saint days, in honor of the Virgen de Fátima (Virgin Mary). Over the following days, visitors are invited to experience dancing, parades, soccer tournaments and more. Two decades ago, Hacienda Uayamon was inspired by a guest to commission the construction of a new church in town. Nuestra Señora de Fátima is now able to host the surrounding area of Campeche during this commemoration of the Virgin.

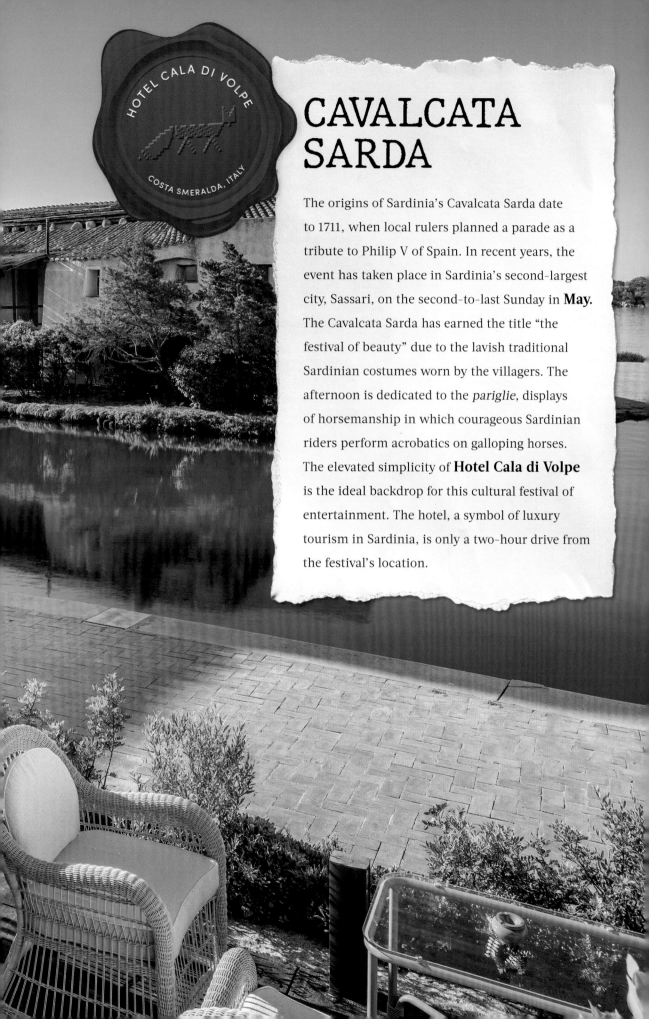

HOTEL CALA DI VOLPE

COSTA SMERALDA, ITALY

CAVALCATA SARDA

The origins of Sardinia's Cavalcata Sarda date to 1711, when local rulers planned a parade as a tribute to Philip V of Spain. In recent years, the event has taken place in Sardinia's second-largest city, Sassari, on the second-to-last Sunday in **May.** The Cavalcata Sarda has earned the title "the festival of beauty" due to the lavish traditional Sardinian costumes worn by the villagers. The afternoon is dedicated to the *pariglie,* displays of horsemanship in which courageous Sardinian riders perform acrobatics on galloping horses. The elevated simplicity of **Hotel Cala di Volpe** is the ideal backdrop for this cultural festival of entertainment. The hotel, a symbol of luxury tourism in Sardinia, is only a two-hour drive from the festival's location.

A KEY TO THE CITY

During Doors Open Minneapolis, which takes place over a weekend in **May,** the public can get a behind-the-scenes look at many beautiful, interesting places in the city that they would not normally be able to see, like the building that used to house Prince's recording studio. Caretakers at these sites provide context as to why the spots, and the people and businesses that work and operate in them, are such marvels. **Hotel Ivy** participates in the festival by hosting a reception and showing off its uniquely beautiful building.

HOTEL IVY

MINNEAPOLIS, MINNESOTA, UNITED STATES

The historic Ivy Tower, built in 1930

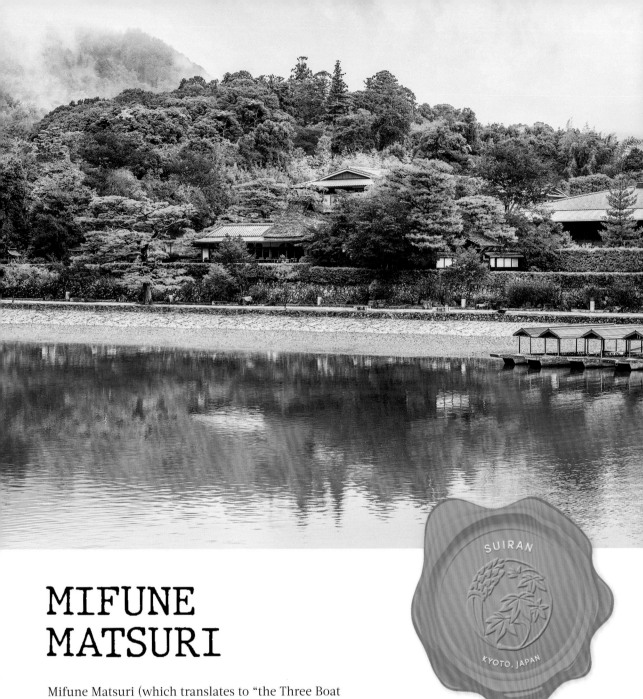

MIFUNE MATSURI

Mifune Matsuri (which translates to "the Three Boat Festival") is hosted in **May** by the Kurumazaki Shrine on the Oi River in Kyoto. The festival began in 1922, and it re-creates the spectacle of pleasure-boating aristocrats during the Heian Era from about a thousand years ago. Poetry recitation, traditional music and dance are performed on traditional boats that resemble dragons. **Suiran,** located right by the bank of the river, offers guests an exclusive viewing area of the festivities and operates as an official sponsor of this event.

SUIRAN

KYOTO, JAPAN

MATILD PALACE

BUDAPEST, HUNGARY

BELVÁROSI FESTIVAL

Music fills the streets of Budapest each **May** during the Belvárosi Festival (Downtown Festival), also known as BelFeszt, marking the beginning of summer and the festival season. This free music festival hosts performances across the city, at locations such as Szabadság tér and Erzsébet tér, two beautiful squares and both just a ten-minute walk from **Matild Palace.** The three-day event offers jazz, rock, pop and folk concerts, thrilling visitors and locals alike.

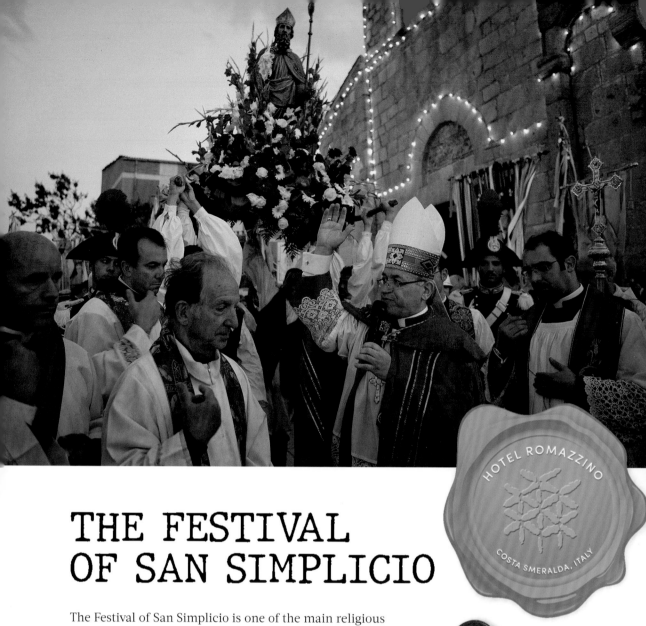

THE FESTIVAL OF SAN SIMPLICIO

The Festival of San Simplicio is one of the main religious festivals in Sardinia, honoring Olbia's patron saint, San Simplicio. Olbia, a beautiful coastal city in the northeast of this island, is near the **Hotel Romazzino** in Costa Smeralda. The festival takes place over a few days each **May** and features numerous equestrian events, food and religious ceremonies. Expect bright fireworks, local cuisine and endless wine! Some not-to-be-missed activities include the Festival of Mussels, in which people feast on the region's specialty, and the Palio della Stella, a horse race where riders try to spear a dangling star while on the hoof.

A traditional procession
through Sardinia during the
Festival of San Simplicio

THE PARK TOWER KNIGHTSBRIDGE

LONDON, ENGLAND

IN FULL BLOOM

Every spring London becomes a veritable riot of color and fragrance as it welcomes the world's leading horticulturalists and floral professionals to the Chelsea Flower Show. Held over five days in **May**, it is attended by a distinguished guest list that includes the British royal family. From the show's humble beginnings in 1862 in a single tent to the five-day extravaganza where garden designers and plant breeders showcase their talents, there is more to enjoy than just the show. There are also shopping opportunities galore and a chance to indulge in some delightful dining options. **The Park Tower Knightsbridge,** a short twenty-minute walk from the show, makes the perfect base from which to explore London and its spring blooms, while offering a selection of floral-inspired cocktails and mocktails using botanical flavors.

DRAGON BOAT FESTIVAL

For over 2,000 years, people in China have commemorated Qu Wan, a celebrated poet and minister, with the traditional Dragon Boat Festival in **May** or June. Among the main features of the festival are the boat races that occur across the country; one such race happens just outside Hunan's capital of Changsha, close to **Meixi Lake Hotel.** Of course, there are delicious things to eat during the festivities–in particular, people enjoy *zongzi*, a pyramid-shaped rice dumpling. One tradition of this festival is the five-colored braid of strings given to children to protect them from demons and bless them with a long life. Wormwood leaves are also hung on doors, and pouches of incense are worn to ward off evil spirits.

MEIXI LAKE HOTEL

CHANGSHA, CHINA

Orchestras performing
during Prague Spring

PRAGUE SPRING

Founded by the renowned conductor Rafael
Kubelík in 1946, Prague Spring is a three-week
classical-music festival with dozens of concerts that
celebrate Czech and international composers. It has
a fine history: The 1946 event was the first occasion
Leonard Bernstein conducted an orchestra outside
of the United States. Held in the Czech Republic's
capital, this event spans **May** and June. Les Clefs d'Or
concierge at **Augustine** is the go-to source to reserve
tickets or receive a recommendation.

YEREVAN WINE DAYS

Each **May**, Armenia's oenophiles head to Saryan Street, a short walk from **The Alexander,** for Yerevan Wine Days in the capital of Armenia. The beautiful central street becomes a hub of up-and-coming wineries and local vintners offering tastings and complimentary bites to attendees. Lively music fills the streets as guests try wines made with local varieties of grapes and sample signature Armenian delicacies.

THE ALEXANDER

YEREVAN, ARMENIA

GAME, SET, MATCH

One of four grand-slam tennis tournaments that take place across the world, Wimbledon is held every summer in **June** or **July**. Many spectators come from all over the globe to witness the world's best players in action, including patrons from the royal family. It's traditional for spectators to nibble on strawberries and cream as they watch the match—this combination was served at the first Wimbledon in 1877—and **The Wellesley Knightsbridge** is proud to serve its own version to guests who stay there during the tournament. The hotel's Les Clefs d'Or concierge can assist guests with acquiring tickets or even provide more exclusive experiences.

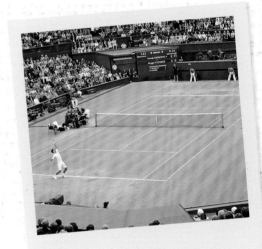

CHOREA GALA

Every **June,** world-class ballet troupes from across the globe gather for the Chorea Gala at an outdoor venue by the Danube River in Bratislava, Slovakia. The goal is to bring together theater companies and dancers from many nations. Guests staying at the **Grand Hotel River Park** have a chance to experience the artistic performances directly from their rooms or suites facing the Grand Plaza. The Grand Hotel River Park is one of the main partners of this event, so it serves as a backdrop for many of the unique performances, while also accommodating the wonderful talents who perform.

GRAND HOTEL RIVER PARK

BRATISLAVA, SLOVAKIA

CARLOS SOUZA
Global Brand Ambassador at Valentino

Q: What is a celebration you can't miss each year?
Being Brazilian, Carnival in Rio de Janeiro.

Q: What makes this celebration special?
It has the best costumes, the best music, the best samba performances, the best dancers.

Q: What is the best way to experience this celebration?
Book a special booth a year in advance at the Sambódromo to experience the feast of color and music where, over the course of two nights, twelve samba schools perform.

Q: What is one of your favorite activities that you've experienced at this celebration?
The music, the costumes, the singing and drums of samba schools with their traditional colors passing in front of you are moments you will never forget.

Q: What are some tips you would give to someone attending this celebration?
The parade will start at nightfall and last until early morning. My suggestion for a good night is to alternate your drinks with a glass of water as the night goes on. It is a very long and colorful night.

THE WINTER SUN

First celebrated by the Incans, Inti Raymi, or Fiesta del Sol, is a celebration of Inti, the sun god. It takes place during the winter solstice in the Southern Hemisphere, usually in **June.** During the festival, numerous participants re-create Incan rites of sun worship at several sites, including Sacsayhuamán, a historic citadel on the outskirts of Cusco, Peru. The ceremonies are done in the Quechua language, and the people dress in traditional costumes. The city of Cusco is transformed into a festival of color. **Palacio del Inka** boasts front-row seats to the ceremony, as it starts in the atrium of the Santo Domingo temple, which is just opposite the hotel.

PALACIO DEL INKA

CUSCO, PERU

THE JOSEPH

NASHVILLE, TENNESSEE, UNITED STATES

CMA FEST

Known as Music City, USA, Nashville hosts the annual Country Music Association Fest each **June.** This festival, attended by more than 80,000 guests, is the ultimate country-music experience, including more than 250 live performances by legendary hitmakers and up-and-coming talents held at the city's top venues, from stadium arenas to intimate stages. **The Joseph's** team is pleased to create music-inspired itineraries for this beloved event.

FIRE-JUMPING IN CRETE

The day of Klidonas is celebrated every year on **June** 24 in Greece. Now linked with St. John, the date was originally tied to honoring the god Apollo, celebrating the sun god on the longest day of the year. The festivities include several unique traditions such as the lighting of bonfires and jumping over them as an act of purification. Guests at **Domes Zeen Chania** can venture to the nearby town of Vamos, which is renowned for its Klidonas celebrations.

DOMES ZEEN CHANIA
CRETE, GREECE

The traditional feast of Klidonas involves adventurous activities

CABARETE KITE FESTIVAL

The Cabarete Kite Festival in **June** celebrates the dynamic water sport known as kiteboarding, in which people glide across the water (and into the air!) on a board, using a kite to harness the power of Dominican Republic winds. But the festival is more than just a celebration of this sport—it also emphasizes entrepreneurship and ocean conservation. As part of the GKA Kite World Tour, the festival features a week of surf sessions, sunset music on the beach and epic kiteboarding. Professional kiteboarders are invited to compete, and viewers can enjoy watching them fly through the air. Furthermore, special guests are invited to share their knowledge on a variety of topics such as health and wellness, tech, sports and ocean conservation. **The Ocean Club** accommodates both spectators and participants during this exciting time.

THE OCEAN CLUB

COSTA NORTE, DOMINICAN REPUBLIC

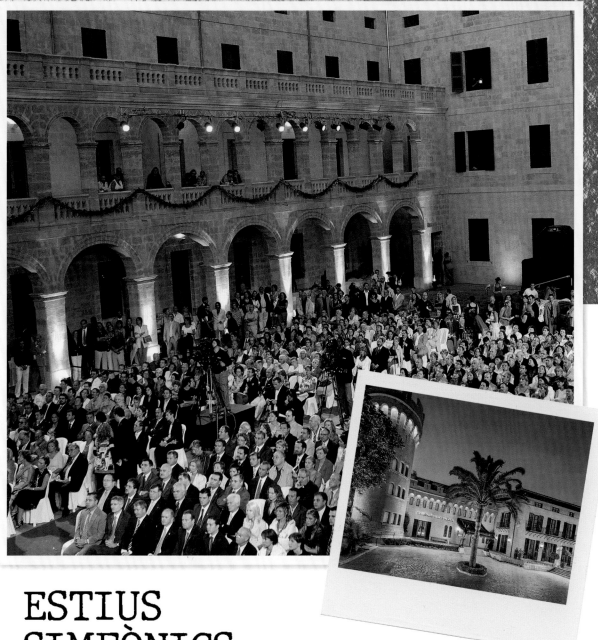

ESTIUS
SIMFÒNICS

Every summer, the Estius Simfònics musical festival fills
the famous Spanish resort island of Mallorca with songs.
The magical performances are held throughout the months
of **June, July** and **August,** when guests can appreciate
the music of internationally known artists in incomparably
beautiful locations, such as La Misericórdia, a historic
cultural center. With **Castillo Hotel Son Vida** located in
Palma, the capital of Mallorca, guests will certainly enjoy
the sights this city has to offer.

CASTILLO HOTEL SON VIDA

MALLORCA, SPAIN

AND THEY'RE OFF...

One of Britain's most famous racecourses, the Ascot holds a special week of races in **June** each year called the Royal Ascot. The most notable attendee was the Queen, who famously loved horses. With prize money of more than £8 million, it is Britain's most popular racing event. In addition to attracting many of the world's finest racehorses to compete, around 300,000 visitors attend every year. It is equally synonymous with sartorial elegance, as guests traditionally wear splendid outfits and hats. Other events worth attending include the Royal Procession, when members of the royal family arrive via horse-drawn carriage, and Singing Around the Bandstand, a communal event that rounds out each day at the races. Guests staying at **The Langley** are invited to start their day of the event with a traditional afternoon tea in the drawing room of the hotel, before departing for the races in style—the hotel offers a luxury chauffeur service.

THE LANGLEY

BUCKINGHAMSHIRE, ENGLAND

JULY
AUGUST
SEPTEMBER

JERASH FESTIVAL

Throughout the month of **July,** Jordan hosts its annual
Jerash Festival, which aims to celebrate the culture of
Jordan. Locals from the region and tourists are invited
to enjoy the live music, food, performances and crafts,
all in the ruins of Jerash, one of the best-preserved
ancient-Roman cities in the world. Join in the
festivities while staying at **Al Manara** in Aqaba.

*Visitors attend a performance at the
South Theater of ancient Jerash*

GION FESTIVAL

The Gion Matsuri is Kyoto's largest festival, spanning the entire month of **July.** The origins of the festival date all the way back to the year 869, as a way to appease the gods during an epidemic. Each year, a local boy is chosen as a sacred messenger to the gods. For four days, his feet never touch the ground, and he sits on one of the many elaborate floats. The festival has two types of floats: *yama* and *hoko*. Both are spectacular, decorated with fabric, dyed textiles and sculptures, but the *hoko* are larger. During the festival, there are two processions in which floats are paraded through downtown. **HOTEL THE MITSUI KYOTO,** located in the heart of Kyoto, embraces the cultural importance of the event.

SAVE THE DATE

In **July,** people from across the United Arab Emirates travel to Liwa to celebrate the importance of the date palm, a beloved and essential local staple. Through competitions, markets and events, the Liwa Date Festival showcases the best local dates. But this festival is not only about the dates—it is also a celebration of traditional Bedouin culture, highlighting the heritage and ancient customs of the United Arab Emirates. The team at **Ajman Saray** are excited to welcome guests at this time and share a taste of the local culture.

AJMAN SARAY

AJMAN, UNITED ARAB EMIRATES

A SENSORY EXPERIENCE

The City of Lights lives up to its name with La Nuit aux Invalides, a spectacular multimedia sound and light show. The presentation is as unique as the venue: it's projected onto the façade of Les Invalides, the historic military building in the heart of the city. A technological achievement, the impressive event has been awing tourists, Parisians and history lovers alike every **July** since 2012. Each year the presentation recounts a different historic tale. Just across the Seine, **Prince de Galles** offers luxurious accommodation to rest one's head after the spectacle and dream of the miraculous lights.

VIVE LA LIBERTÉ

The French national holiday Bastille Day, on **July** 14, is a massive party, and it starts with a military parade on the Champs-Élysées. The sound of trumpets and bugles marks the arrival of the French president at the top of the world's most famous avenue. Elite units of the French army parade down the avenue, which is always lined with crowds of onlookers. **Hôtel de Berri Champs-Élysées,** built on the site of designer Elsa Schiaparelli's former home, offers a front-row seat to the parade during the day and, by night, the impressive fireworks display.

A display of fireworks on Bastille Day

Musical performances entertain guests at the International Gümüslük Music Festival

MUSICAL BODRUM

Music lovers descend upon the small fishing village of Gümüşlük in Turkey each **July** to attend the International Gümüşlük Music Festival. World-renowned performances are held at the magnificent Ancient Stone Quarry in Koyunbaba and at nearby hotels and restaurants along the Bodrum peninsula. With the festival taking place over the course of two months, guests of the **Caresse Bodrum** hotel can enjoy a prolonged stay, experiencing the best of Turkey's cultural and natural abundance.

CARESSE BODRUM

BODRUM, TURKEY

SAMUI REGATTA

Over four days each **July,** the Samui Regatta hosts a series of exciting boat races. Since the inaugural event in 2002, it has become a highly competitive and well-regarded regatta, cementing Koh Samui's reputation as one of the best sailing destinations in the region. It wouldn't be a regatta without parties, and many of them happen between sailing events. **Vana Belle** is conveniently located along Chaweng Beach, where many of the competitions take place.

VANA BELLE

KOH SAMUI, THAILAND

CHERRY CREEK ARTS FESTIVAL

HOTEL CLIO

DENVER, COLORADO, UNITED STATES

Held annually during the first weekend of **July,** the Cherry Creek Arts Festival is a three-day celebration of visual, culinary and performing arts. Carefully curated exhibits provide a platform to showcase work from 250 of America's top visual artists. It's an event for all ages: Children can participate in "artivities," such as making statues out of vegetables. The festival is Colorado's signature cultural event and a nationally renowned art festival, attracting approximately 150,000 people yearly. **Hotel Clio** is at the epicenter of the festivities, located within walking distance of the festival grounds, so guests can fully immerse themselves.

One-of-a-kind performers participate in the celebration

RIA FORMOSA

Many seafood lovers choose to book their trips to Algarve in **July** to attend the Ria Formosa Festival. Ria Formosa is such a beautiful coastal lagoon that it was voted one of the Seven Natural Wonders of Portugal by the Portuguese people in a recent poll. This area also happens to be the source of some of the best seafood in the country. The town that hosts the festival, Faro, is a short drive from **Pine Cliffs Resort,** so this gastronomic event is easily accessible to guests.

PINE CLIFFS RESORT

ALGARVE, PORTUGAL

IN MOTION

For ten days every **July,** the Kalamata Dance Festival offers a celebration of dance and music, with performances by leading Greek and international artists. The festival features daily shows at the city's dance hall, known as the Dance Megaron, and outdoor performances in the city's central square. Guests at **The Romanos** are able to experience this major dance event by watching daily video projections or attending the live dance performances on the premises.

THE ROMANOS

COSTA NAVARINO, GREECE

Thrilling live dance performances abound during this festival

WHITE NIGHT

The White City of Tel Aviv is a UNESCO World Heritage site in architecture for its many examples of early-twentieth-century Bauhaus structures. Each year on the evening of June 30 and stretching into the early hours of **July** 1, the city celebrates with special White City festivities called White Night. Visitors arrive to experience unique nighttime attractions where the city turns into a celebration of music, color and movement, with most sites free of charge and open until dawn. Visitors can attend a variety of events, including concerts, theater shows, dance festivals and markets such as the Jaffa Flea Market. Galleries and museums, like the Ilana Goor Museum and the famous Uri Geller Museum in the Old City of Jaffa, are located just steps from **The Jaffa.** Guests at the Jaffa relax in modern luxury within an exquisitely restored nineteenth-century building, and only need to step outside to enjoy the vibrant festivities.

COMIC-CON

Since its first convention, held in 1970,
Comic-Con International has become the largest
pop-culture event in the United States and one
of the signature summer events in San Diego.
Thousands of artists, celebrities and fans of comic
books come together over their shared passion
for four days every **July. THE US GRANT** has
a long history with Comic-Con, as the inaugural
location of this iconic fair.

SALZBURG FESTIVAL

The Salzburg Festival is one of the most prominent festivals of opera, classical music and drama in the world, held in the notably musical Austrian city of Salzburg, where Wolfgang Amadeus Mozart was born. The festival was established in 1920; it starts in **July** every year and runs for five weeks. Guests are able to enjoy a wide range of operas, plays and concerts, including many activities for young people. **Hotel Goldener Hirsch** is conveniently located near many of the performance halls and in close proximity to several of the landmarks that pay homage to Mozart, such as the Mozartplatz and House for Mozart, allowing guests to explore Salzburg's musical heritage.

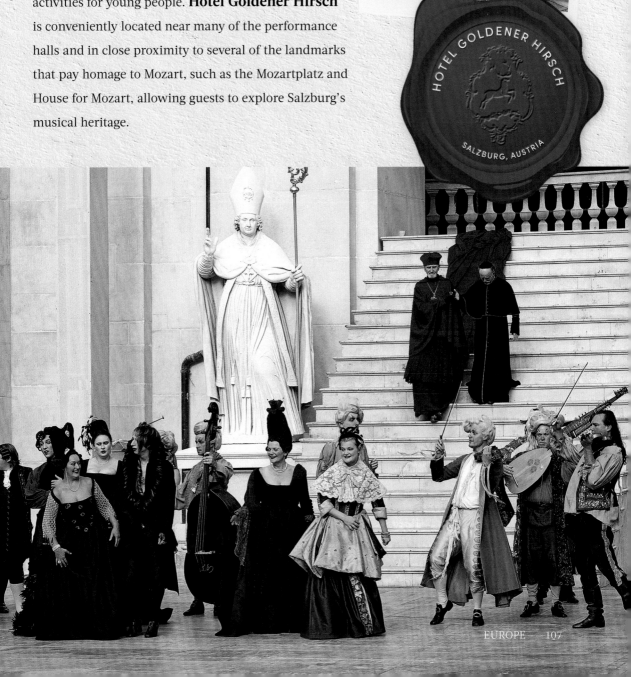

ISLAND OF JAZZ

Situated in the north of Sardinia, a leisurely drive from Costa Smeralda's **Hotel Pitrizza,** is the town of Berchidda, where the famed jazz musician Paolo Fresu was born. To honor his hometown and his passion for jazz music, Fresu founded the Time in Jazz Festival, which takes place each **August** in Sardinia. Events are held in the main square of Berchidda, in the surrounding forest and in small churches in the neighboring areas. The sounds of jazz entice more than 40,000 fans to this Italian island each year.

HOTEL PITRIZZA
COSTA SMERALDA, ITALY

VIRGEN DE LA ASUNCIÓN

To commemorate the Assumption, on **August** 15, the day the Virgin Mary ascended to heaven in Catholic tradition, people celebrate the Virgen de la Asunción festival with parades, food and games. Traditionally, locals pray to the Virgin Mary for miracles during this time. Guests at **Hacienda Temozón** can mingle with locals and enjoy the festivities.

HACIENDA TEMOZÓN

TEMOZÓN SUR, MEXICO

FULL-MOON CONCERT

On the night of the full moon in **August,** a multitude of archaeological sites, museums and monuments in Greece welcome guests with a wide variety of events after normal visiting hours. One of these events is a concert hosted on the uninhabited Delos Island, which was sacred to the ancient Greeks and is home to extensive ruins. This program includes music with lyrics from historical poetry and theater. The team at Mykonos's **Santa Marina** will gladly arrange private water transportation for guests wishing to attend the cultural evening on this UNESCO World Heritage site.

Kato Mili windmills in Mykonos

THE VARKAROLA

Held every summer on the Greek island of Corfu, the Varkarola Festival celebrates the miracle of Saint Spyridon. According to the tale, the saint saved the island from a Turkish siege on **August** 11, 1716. To commemorate this miracle, a mock nautical fight is held during the festival, in which boats parade along the bay of Paleokastritsa while people perform traditional music and dances. At the end of the festival, a boat is set on fire to symbolize the defeat of the enemy forces, with fireworks for a grand finale. Guests at **Domes Miramare** are able to enjoy the fireworks from the comfort of their rooms.

DOMES MIRAMARE

CORFU, GREECE

COSME

COSME
PAROS

PAROS, GREECE

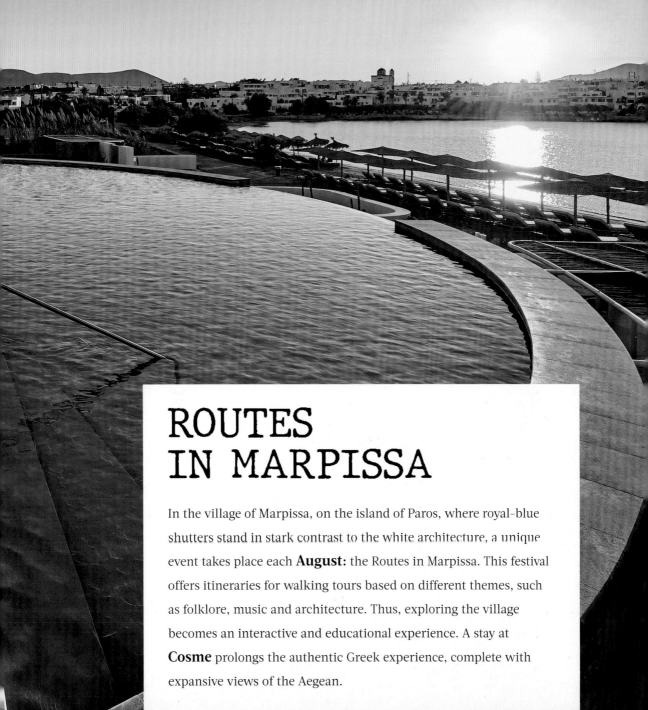

ROUTES
IN MARPISSA

In the village of Marpissa, on the island of Paros, where royal-blue shutters stand in stark contrast to the white architecture, a unique event takes place each **August:** the Routes in Marpissa. This festival offers itineraries for walking tours based on different themes, such as folklore, music and architecture. Thus, exploring the village becomes an interactive and educational experience. A stay at **Cosme** prolongs the authentic Greek experience, complete with expansive views of the Aegean.

GANESH CHATURTHI

One of the most important Hindu festivals in Mumbai's calendar, Ganesh Chaturthi is dedicated to Ganesh, the elephant-headed god, who is believed to remove obstacles from his disciples' path. The festival is celebrated over ten days in **August** to commemorate Ganesh's birth; many communities place clay idols in elaborate tents known as pandals. **ITC Maratha's** concierge curates special trips for guests during this festival, often working with local organizers to ensure guests can easily enter to see the idol. The restaurant Peshwa Pavilion offers guests a special menu of local delicacies as well.

LOS CABOS OPEN

The Los Cabos Open, held on Mexico's Baja California peninsula each **August,** is a tennis extravaganza. **Solaz** resort has played a prominent role in the success of the event, serving as the main sponsor and the headquarters hotel, and hosting all the players who have participated in the tournament. In 2020, the hotel built first-class tennis facilities featuring the main stadium of the Los Cabos Open, with a capacity of 3,500 spectators. Solaz resort is the center of the notable social gatherings during the tournament, including the kickoff party, the players' pool party and the closing party.

ANOTHER ROUND!

To combat the summer heat in July or **August,** more than thirty beer vendors set up tents at the vast Dalian Xinghai Square to participate in the Dalian International Beer Festival. Here, domestic and foreign beer makers showcase hundreds of types of beer, attracting millions of tourists. Every beer house has its own characteristics, so visitors wend their way among them while also attending the beer carnival, the photography competition, the drinking competition and other themed activities. The Royal Cellar restaurant in **The Castle Hotel** invites guests to try its signature house-brewed beer under a promotion that coincides with the festival.

CHEERS!

Cyprus has been producing wine for nearly 6,000 years. The city of Limassol celebrates this heritage for two weeks every **August** and **September** during the Limassol Wine Festival. A feature of the local calendar since 1961, the festival includes music, dancing, food, fireworks displays, singing, traditional grape stomping and, of course, plenty of wine! The Wine Festival is held at the Limassol Municipal Garden, which is located a short distance from the **Parklane.** Guests who aren't able to attend can still enjoy a wide selection of local and international wines at the resort's Gallery lounge, which overlooks the glistening waters of the Mediterranean Sea.

Revelers enjoy the endless flow of wine and the celebratory atmosphere

PARKLANE

LIMASSOL, CYPRUS

LIVING ON THE EDGE

BLUE PALACE ELOUNDA

CRETE, GREECE

Along Crete's breathtaking coast, at a height of twenty meters, each **September** athletes participate in a cliff-diving competition, while onlookers gaze in amazement. In Agios Nikolaos, the best of the best are invited to dive from the natural cliffs into the glistening waters of Lake Voulismeni below. Guests of **Blue Palace Elounda** can take a short, scenic drive along the coast to experience the adventurous event firsthand and the accompanying festivities, including live music, art shows, fireworks, food and drinks.

Diving into the glistening waters of Lake Voulismeni

FIONA LEAHY
Creative director and event designer

Q: What is the best dish you've tried at a celebration?

At the Carnival of Venice, I tried *frittelle* for the first time, a Venetian doughnut–delicious sugared fried balls of dough with pine nuts and raisins. I still dream of them.

Q: What is the best souvenir you have gotten from a celebration?

I bought a bespoke leather mask from one of the oldest mask makers in Venice–a piece of wonderful craft and beauty. I still have it hanging on the wall of my dressing room.

Q: What are some tips you would give to someone attending your favorite celebration?

I would say first to book accommodation far in advance, as Carnival in Venice is a popular celebration. I would recommend attending a ball. These can be booked ahead of time as well, and I would recommend renting a theatrical costume so you feel and look the part.

Q: How would you describe your favorite celebration/festival in three words?

A visually decadent, historical celebration. (Five words–sorry!)

The Warsaw Autumn Festival has a
rich history spanning several decades

AUTUMN FESTIVAL

Every **September,** musicians from around the world visit Warsaw to be a part of one of the best musical events in the country: the Warsaw Autumn Festival. For about eight days, visitors can attend various performances, concerts and operas, as well as participate in interactive events such as workshops, meetings and installations. Because the festival takes place across different institutions, churches, universities, radio stations, museums and orchestra houses in Warsaw, guests at **Hotel Bristol** are right in the center of the action.

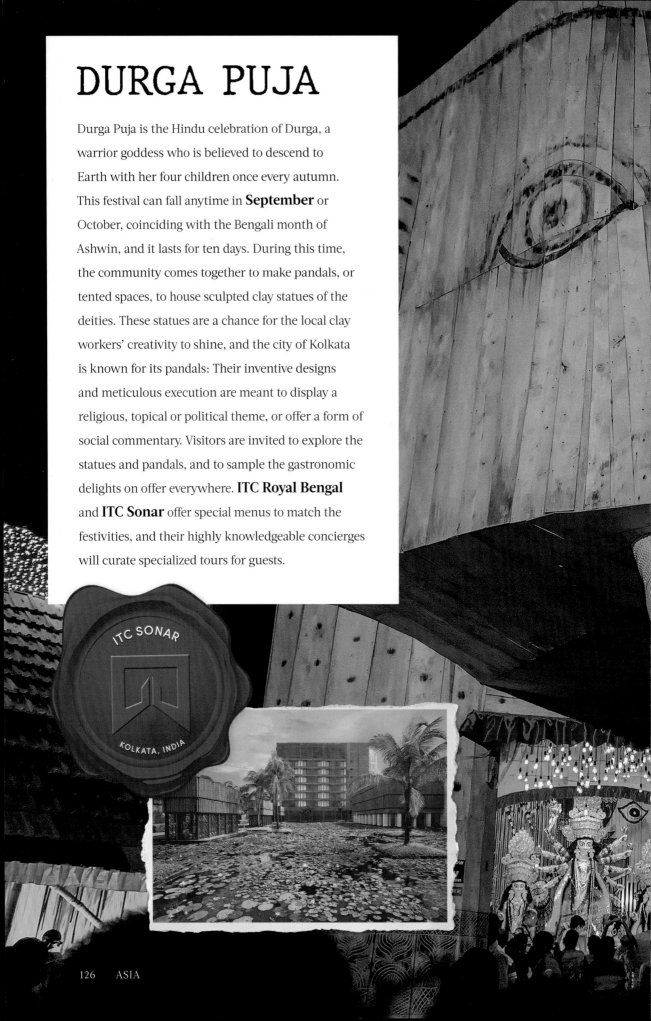

DURGA PUJA

Durga Puja is the Hindu celebration of Durga, a warrior goddess who is believed to descend to Earth with her four children once every autumn. This festival can fall anytime in **September** or October, coinciding with the Bengali month of Ashwin, and it lasts for ten days. During this time, the community comes together to make pandals, or tented spaces, to house sculpted clay statues of the deities. These statues are a chance for the local clay workers' creativity to shine, and the city of Kolkata is known for its pandals: Their inventive designs and meticulous execution are meant to display a religious, topical or political theme, or offer a form of social commentary. Visitors are invited to explore the statues and pandals, and to sample the gastronomic delights on offer everywhere. **ITC Royal Bengal** and **ITC Sonar** offer special menus to match the festivities, and their highly knowledgeable concierges will curate specialized tours for guests.

ITC SONAR

KOLKATA, INDIA

ITC ROYAL BENGAL

KOLKATA, INDIA

OSMANTHUS CITY FLOWER FESTIVAL

THE AZURE QIANTANG
HANGZHOU, CHINA

Sweet-scented Osmanthus, native to eastern Asia

Osmanthus is the official flower of Hangzhou and noted for its fragrance and medicinal properties. When it blooms in **September** and October, the city hosts a monthlong Osmanthus Festival, where guests are invited to stroll along the flower-filled paths, drink Osmanthus tea and attend art exhibitions. **The Azure Qiantang** partners up with a local tea company to offer a tour for hotel guests to learn more of the history.

THE HONGTA HOTEL
SHANGHAI, CHINA

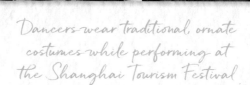

Dancers wear traditional, ornate costumes while performing at the Shanghai Tourism Festival

VISIT SHANGHAI

Since its inauguration in 1990, the Shanghai Tourism Festival has been a witness to China's development. Held in **September,** the festival serves as an opportunity for locals and foreigners to explore Chinese culture and history. Guests can enjoy performances by dance troupes from across the globe, a parade and a folk-culture exhibition, among other events. As the designated hotel for the festival, **the Hongta Hotel** allows guests to purchase discounted tickets through its concierge.

ART ATHINA

Art Athina is one of the most prestigious contemporary art shows in Greece–it's also one of the oldest in Europe, having started in 1993. Often taking place in **September,** it gathers gallerists from Greece and abroad in a celebration of artists in all fields. **King George** has a special connection to the festival: It has previously hosted a pop-up exhibition within its lobby for guests to fully immerse themselves in this celebratory period.

KING GEORGE

ATHENS, GREECE

IFESTIA FESTIVAL

A celebration with historic ties, the Ifestia Festival commemorates the
volcano eruption that changed the landscape of Santorini around 1600 BCE.
Every **September,** Santorini hosts concerts, art exhibitions and dance
performances to honor the majesty of nature. The highlight of the festival
is the spectacular re-creation of the volcanic eruption with fireworks.
Mystique is itself an ode to this volcanic island, so what better place to
stay to experience the pyrotechnics?

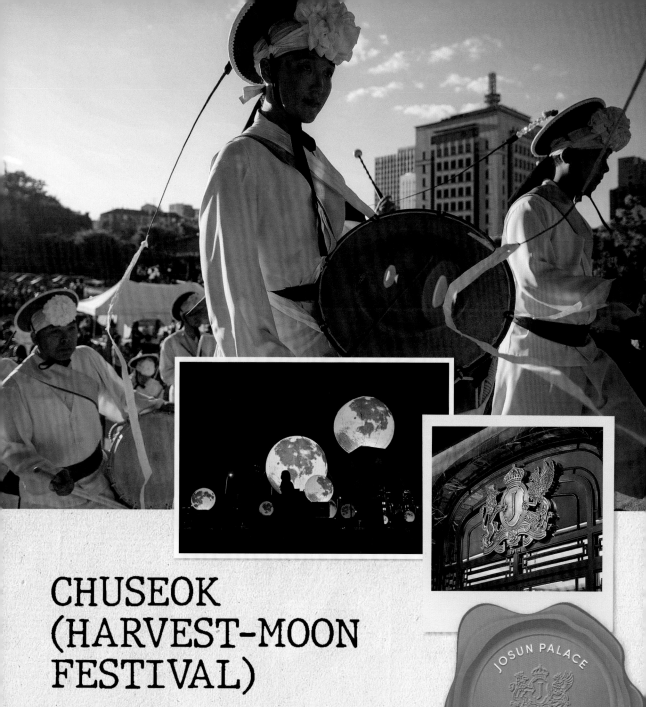

CHUSEOK (HARVEST-MOON FESTIVAL)

Chuseok, also known as Hangawi, is a major South Korean harvest festival celebrated in **September** or October. During Chuseok, people enjoy special foods, particularly a rice cake called *songpyeon*. The dough is made with finely ground rice that is kneaded into small round shapes and filled with delicious things like sesame seeds, chestnuts or red beans. The rice cakes are then steamed on layers of pine needles, filling homes with a delicate, fresh fragrance. **Josun Palace** in Seoul is conveniently located in the heart of the festivities.

LIGHTS, CAMERA, ACTION

The Venice Film Festival has been held annually in late **August** or early **September** since the 1930s, making it the world's oldest film festival. It brings some of the most prominent directors and actors to the red carpet at the Lido di Venezia with viewings of world-class movies. **The Gritti Palace** has a long history with cinema, having hosted many actors and directors. The hotel itself has even appeared in films. Visitors can appreciate this for themselves by looking at the Golden Book, which contains signatures from esteemed guests, and by admiring the collection of portraits along the lobby's Wall of Celebrities, including those of Elizabeth Taylor, Bette Davis and Humphrey Bogart, to name a few. In addition to the Golden Book and the Cinema Corridor, there is a unique suite named after the festival's Coppa Volpi award, which recognizes the best actor/actress. During the festival, the concierge at The Gritti Palace helps guests book their tickets to shows and parties, and will arrange water-taxi transportation to explore the festival.

FIESTAS DE LA VENDIMIA

Fiestas de la Vendimia, or wine festivals, abound during the month of **September** throughout Spain. Las Fiestas de San Mateo, named after Saint Matthew, is the local festival in Logroño, a town in the famous province of Rioja. The festival starts with a bang–literally. Festival organizers set off a rocket, called a *chupinazo,* in the town-hall square. A whole week dedicated to the celebration follows. Once the fiesta has officially begun, the Gran Via wine fountain shoots streams of red, white and rosé wine. There are fireworks, bullfights, food fights and grape stomping. Guests of **Hotel Marqués de Riscal** can participate in a guided tour of the winery and learn about the entire wine-making process.

Giant figures parade through central Logroño

BJÖRN WALLANDER
Photographer

Q: What is one of your favorite celebrations?

Midsummer in Sweden!

Q: What is one of your favorite activities that you've experienced at a party?

Live performances by great musicians.

Q: What makes a party memorable?

The hosts, the guests, the conversations, the music. All of it. Definitely how much of an effort people make to dress up. I think that can set the tone early on.

Q: How do you celebrate personal moments of joy?

Going sailing, riding my motorcycle somewhere with a few friends or a small party for friends in the country.

Q: What are everyday moments that you think people should celebrate more?

Life in general. Wake up and be thankful we are here. Find special places to visit close to where you live. You do not need to travel to the other side of the planet to find joy.

The delectable spread on offer at Feast Portland

LET'S EAT

Every **September** since 2012, gourmands have flocked to Portland, Oregon, to experience Feast Portland, a three-day festival that celebrates all things food and drink, with events that range from intimate drink tastings to large-scale food sampling. The only thing guests have to worry about is pacing themselves. Not only does **The Nines** offer special rates for attendees but the hotel's chefs also participate in various feast events.

THE NINES

PORTLAND, OREGON, UNITED STATES

OCTOBER
NOVEMBER
DECEMBER

BARCOLANA REGATTA

Every second Sunday of **October,** in the Gulf of Trieste, the yacht club Società Velica di Barcola e Grignano holds its historic Barcolana sailing regatta. In 2018, Guinness World Records named it the biggest regatta in the world, with 2,689 boats at the starting line–proving its immense popularity. Guests at the **Falisia Resort,** located right at the gulf, can easily access all the events held during the celebration.

VIENNALE

Hosted every **October** since 1960, the Viennale International Film Festival is Austria's preeminent film event. Here, viewers can see a wide range of films in many of Vienna's vintage cinemas, including experimental movies, short films and documentaries from across the globe. Special events, parties, gala screenings and audience discussions are also held during this period, offering visitors an interactive experience. With **Hotel Bristol** located right in the center of Vienna, guests can participate in the various events and connect with fellow film enthusiasts.

TASTE OF CHARLOTTE

Experience all the amazing dining options Charlotte, North Carolina, has to offer at the Taste of Charlotte, held over three days in September or **October.** Various cafés, restaurants and food trucks in the area provide plenty of tasty bites, accompanied by live musical performances. This culinary event is a great example of North Carolina's famous Southern hospitality, an ethos **The Ballantyne** prizes–and it's happy to greet guests after a day of feasting.

THE BALLANTYNE

CHARLOTTE, NORTH CAROLINA, UNITED STATES

IRAPH SUI

MIYAKO, JAPAN

PAANTU

Named after a supernatural god that brings good luck and
wards off evil spirits, the festival of Paantu takes place on the
island of Miyakojima in Japan's southernmost prefecture of
Okinawa. It follows the Japanese lunar calendar, but is generally held in **October.**
Islanders dress up as the being in branches, leaves and thick layers of mud, and
then walk around town to spread the mud onto newly built houses, the faces
of newborn children and other places to bless them with good luck. UNESCO's
Intangible Cultural Heritage List has recognized the festival, and **Iraph Sui**
encourages guests to participate and spread the mud.

NIGHT OF
THE MUSEUMS

Buenos Aires is one of the cultural capitals of the world, and for one night each **October** or November, people can access many of its riches for free. On Museum Night, between eight p.m. and three a.m., over 240 museums and cultural spaces open their doors to the public, all completely free. For more than fifteen years, this evening has offered a unique way to see some of the most impressive collections and exhibitions in the city. The **Park Tower** is ideally situated for visitors to see many of the best museums and landmarks.

PARK TOWER

BUENOS AIRES, ARGENTINA

PICNIC IN THE PARK

Phil the Park is the largest outdoor musical event in Savannah, Georgia, hosted by the Savannah Philharmonic Orchestra in **October.** The 20,000 attendees converge in picturesque Forsyth Park, the largest public park in Savannah's Historic District. Visitors are encouraged to pack a picnic or purchase dinner from one of the food trucks at the event, and then listen to music from local artists. The concierge at **Perry Lane Hotel** is the ideal curator for a custom picnic basket or to arrange for a Perry Lane Luxury Picnic–an elevated setup for the main event.

PERRY LANE HOTEL

SAVANNAH, GEORGIA, UNITED STATES

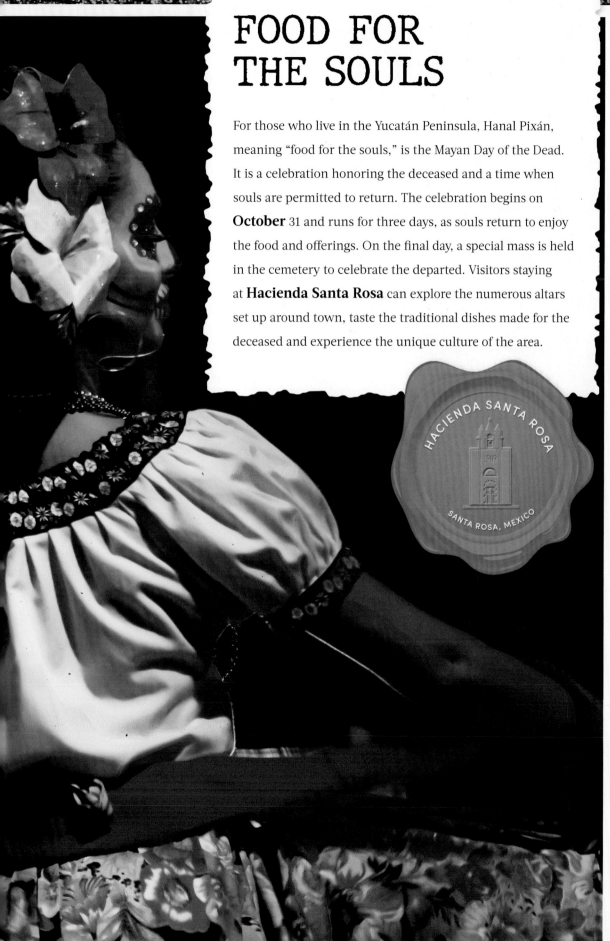

FOOD FOR THE SOULS

For those who live in the Yucatán Peninsula, Hanal Pixán, meaning "food for the souls," is the Mayan Day of the Dead. It is a celebration honoring the deceased and a time when souls are permitted to return. The celebration begins on **October** 31 and runs for three days, as souls return to enjoy the food and offerings. On the final day, a special mass is held in the cemetery to celebrate the departed. Visitors staying at **Hacienda Santa Rosa** can explore the numerous altars set up around town, taste the traditional dishes made for the deceased and experience the unique culture of the area.

HACIENDA SANTA ROSA

SANTA ROSA, MEXICO

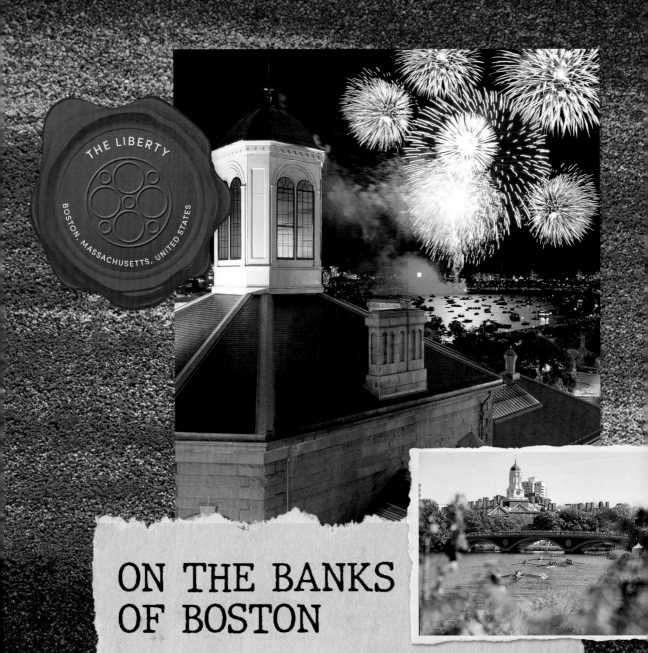

ON THE BANKS OF BOSTON

The Head of the Charles Regatta is one of Boston's greatest traditions, happening on the third weekend of **October.** This elite rowing event started in 1965 and is now the largest two-day race in the world, bringing more than 11,000 athletes to Boston every year. The three-mile race has several twists and turns, and crews can be penalized for steering the course incorrectly. The regatta offers the 300,000 spectators a variety of activities, from watching the race at the Reunion Village to enjoying local cuisine at the Weld Exhibition, one of the pavilions. **The Liberty** hotel, set right in Beacon Hill near the Charles River, offers guests easy access to the Reunion Village, or guests can enjoy the local cuisine at the Liberty's CLINK or Scampo restaurants.

DIWALI

The Hindu Festival of Lights, known as Diwali, celebrates Lord Rama's triumphant return to his kingdom after vanquishing the forces of evil. It's celebrated every autumn, typically falling in **October** or November. This is the most important festival for Hindus all over North India. Homes and shops are illuminated with twinkling lights, new clothes are bought, gifts are exchanged and families gather to feast and enjoy each other's company. The **ITC Grand Bharat** decorates its entire space with colorful flowers and creates special menus to match the occasion. Guests are invited to release eco-friendly lanterns and light clay lamps that glow warmly in the evening.

ITC GRAND BHARAT

NEW DELHI, INDIA

CREOLE FESTIVAL

The Creole Festival in the Seychelles is an annual
celebration of the country's culture and traditions,
held in the last week of **October.** Visitors and
guests staying at **North Island** are exposed to
the Creole way of life through cuisine inspired
by its flavors. Other events on the Creole Festival
program include a carnival and workshops on how
to speak the Creole language.

ANKARA FILM

Each **November,** talented filmmakers descend upon Turkey's capital for the Ankara International Film Festival. With screenings of feature films, short films and documentaries, from both Turkish and international filmmakers, there is something for everyone. Ankara used to be the heart of the Turkish film industry, so filmmaking is held in high esteem in this region. The concierge at **Lugal** is always happy to help arrange for guests to attend the festival.

HERITAGE FESTIVAL

Named in honor of the late Sheikh Zayed bin Sultan Al Nahyan, founding father of the United Arab Emirates, the Sheikh Zayed Heritage Festival in Abu Dhabi celebrates the culture of the United Arab Emirates, showcasing its diverse traditions and educating visitors about the legacy of the nation's founder. Thousands of visitors flock to experience the entertainment on offer, including an Arabian horse show, camel racing and falconry shows. The festival starts in **November** and lasts a number of months. **Al Wathba** is close to the festival, and the hotel's concierge can share insight and arrange for transportation to ensure guests have a memorable time.

Students performing during the Karnataka Rajyotsava celebration at Kanteerava Stadium

RAJYOTSAVA

Rajyotsava, meaning "state festival," is celebrated on **November** 1, commemorating the day when the state of Karnataka was created in India in 1956. In celebration, many people hoist the Karnataka flag and sing the state anthem. People will also stage performances of classical Carnatic music, a style popular in southern India. For the occasion, the Cubbon Pavilion at Bengaluru's **ITC Gardenia** honors the anniversary by offering authentic local cuisine.

LOY KRATHONG

Loy Krathong, the Festival of Lights, is generally celebrated in **November** throughout Thailand (the timing varies according to the lunar calendar). Traditionally, *krathong,* or buoyant baskets, are made from banana-tree wood and elaborately decorated with flowers, incense and candles. These are then launched in rivers to show respect for the River Goddess, Phra Mae Khongkha. This ritual is believed to bring good fortune in the coming year. According to Thai legend, the festival originated in Sukhothai, a small town north of Bangkok. During their stay at **The Athenee Hotel,** guests can visit the village to watch the colorful processions and dance performances.

THE ATHENEE HOTEL

BANGKOK, THAILAND

DÍA DE LOS MUERTOS

On **November** 1 and 2, cities in Mexico become inundated with a beautiful yellow flower, called the *cempazuchitl*, and colorful skulls, called *catrinas*, in celebration of Día de los Muertos, or Day of the Dead. During this time, personal offerings, flowers and foods are placed on altars to honor the dead. The festivities are not complete without a taste of freshly baked *pan de muerto*, a sweet bread with a hint of orange blossom. **Las Alcobas** constructs an altar that the hotel's pastry chefs help to decorate with artistic skulls. Taking part in this celebration is an immersion into the vibrant culture of Mexico.

LAS ALCOBAS

MEXICO CITY, MEXICO

The cempazuchitl abounds in Mexico City during Día de los Muertos

STEP INTO TOKYO

Tokyo Heritage Week, held annually in October or
November, offers a chance for people to better
understand the history and culture of Japan. During
the week, visitors can partake in cultural events
such as exhibitions, walking tours and lectures, all
held throughout different neighborhoods in Tokyo.
One of the highlights during this festival is the
opening of the Akasaka Prince Classic House to the
public. This Tudor-style building was built in 1930
as a palace. The house is preserved in its original
glory in the center of Tokyo, and since it's an annex
to **The Prince Gallery Tokyo Kioicho,** guests
can easily visit this historic building.

THE PRINCE GALLERY TOKYO KIOICHO

TOKYO, JAPAN

THE TASMAN

HOBART, AUSTRALIA

SET SAIL!

The Rolex Sydney Hobart Yacht Race starts in Sydney on Boxing Day, **December** 26, and finishes 628 nautical miles later in Hobart, Tasmania. Each year, hundreds of thousands of people line Sydney Harbor to cheer the departing yachts as they sail through Sydney Heads before turning south. Days later, in Hobart, the excitement builds as people wait to see which boat will be the first to arrive. Guests of **The Tasman** are immersed in all the excitement while being in close proximity to the Hobart Race Village. As part of the festivities, there is a packed program of entertainment, food, drinks and family fun.

MERRY MARINA

Cap Cana, Dominican Republic, starts the Christmas season with an annual Boat Parade, held the first Friday of **December.** Festive decorations and colorful lights adorn the boats lining the Cap Cana Marina. The stage is then set for a night of performances with live music, Christmas carols and holiday characters. Guests of **Sanctuary Cap Cana** are whisked away to spend a magical night at the most famous marina in the Caribbean.

MARGHERITA MISSONI
Fashion designer

Q: What is a celebration you can't miss each year?

Holi in Rajasthan is definitely one not to miss.

Q: Is there a unique tradition that you've experienced at a local celebration?

The colors of Holi are one of a kind.

Q: What is the most unusual celebration that you've attended?

Diwali in India. The candle-lighting ceremony is just magical.

Q: What is the best dish you've tried at a celebration?

Chiacchiere are delicious. During Carnival, we always eat them: Fun fact: The name "*chiacchiere*" has over thirty variations just in Italy!

Q: What is the best souvenir you have gotten from a celebration?

The stained, formerly white dress after Holi.

Q: How would you describe your favorite celebration in three words?

Joy, closeness and high energy.

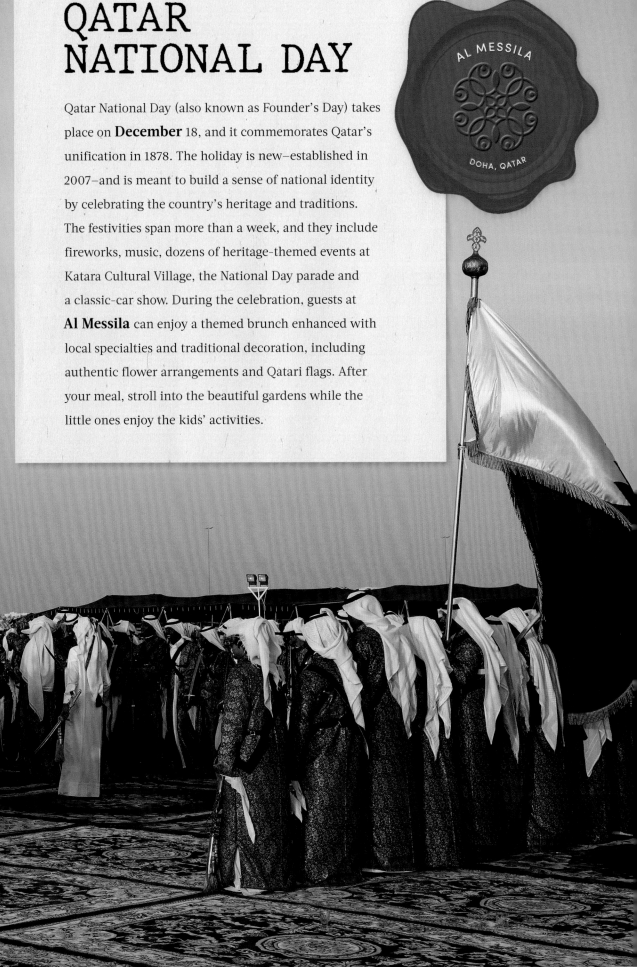

QATAR NATIONAL DAY

Qatar National Day (also known as Founder's Day) takes place on **December** 18, and it commemorates Qatar's unification in 1878. The holiday is new—established in 2007—and is meant to build a sense of national identity by celebrating the country's heritage and traditions. The festivities span more than a week, and they include fireworks, music, dozens of heritage-themed events at Katara Cultural Village, the National Day parade and a classic-car show. During the celebration, guests at **Al Messila** can enjoy a themed brunch enhanced with local specialties and traditional decoration, including authentic flower arrangements and Qatari flags. After your meal, stroll into the beautiful gardens while the little ones enjoy the kids' activities.

AL MESSILA

DOHA, QATAR

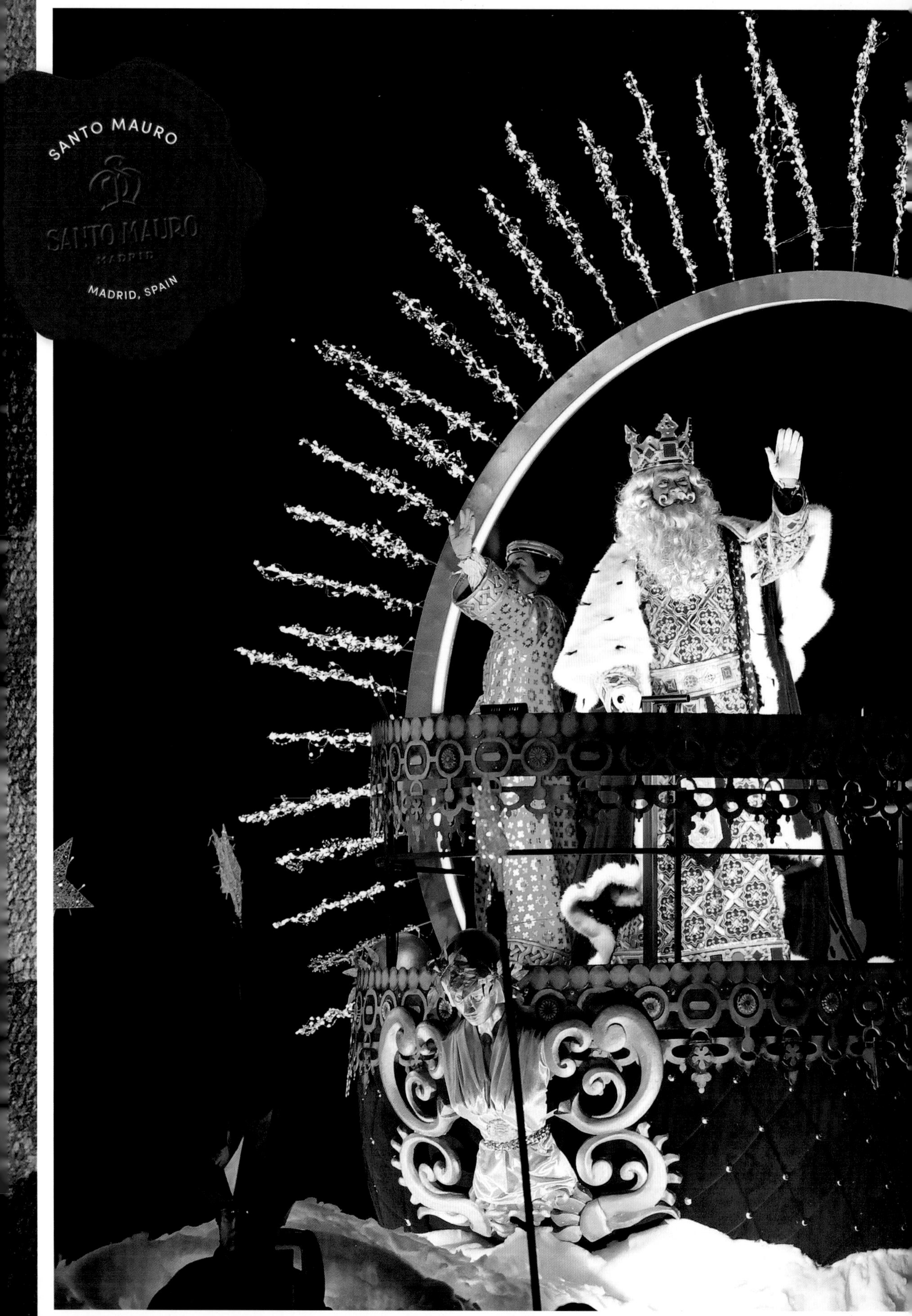
SANTO MAURO
SANTO MAURO
MADRID
MADRID, SPAIN

NAVIDAD

In Madrid, Christmas is not a mere twenty-four-hour event–festivities run from November through **December** and into early January. The Navidad season involves a number of activities across the city, from the Christmas lighting, or *encendido,* at the end of November to touring the Nativity scenes at different churches or the Christmas market in Plaza Mayor. Everyone attending the New Year's Eve celebration at the main square of Puerta del Sol takes part in the tradition of eating twelve grapes for each bell ring as the clock strikes midnight, to bring luck and prosperity in the new year. Guests at **Santo Mauro** can enjoy the traditional Roscón de Reyes, a typical sweet brioche offered on the evening of January 6 to celebrate the arrival of the Three Kings.

UAE NATIONAL DAY

The United Arab Emirates comes alive in a spectacle of red, white, green and black as the nation celebrates its National Day annually on **December** 2. Dubai's **Grosvenor House** is adorned with the national colors, and it houses guests arriving for the festivities. Guests are invited to enjoy the warm December sun before ending the day with a beautiful fireworks display.

GROSVENOR HOUSE

DUBAI, UNITED ARAB EMIRATES

FÊTE DE L'ESCALADE

According to Genevese legend, in 1602, troops sent by the Duke of Savoy were forced to retreat from their attack on Geneva when a local housewife known as Mère Royaume dumped boiling soup on the invaders. This event is commemorated each **December** with the Fête de l'Escalade. One of the most notable events is the parade, which features people in period costumes, transporting visitors back in time. During the celebration, **Hotel President Wilson** displays a traditional chocolate cauldron (*marmite en chocolat*), filled with marzipan and candies, at its weekend brunch.

The chocolate marmite, or cauldron, is a favorite sweet treat enjoyed during the Fête de l'Escalade

LOS TRES REYES

Feria de Reyes originates from an ancient Mayan celebration that commemorates three deities: rain, agriculture and wind. Following the institution of the Franciscan convent, the celebration morphed to celebrate the Three Wise Men: Balthazar, Gaspar and Melchior. The preliminary activities begin in late **December** with the choosing of the queen, who will lead the celebration. Then, starting on December 28, the statues of the Wise Men are moved from niches in the church to a prominent spot on the main altar. On January 6, villagers take them on a village-wide procession, after which the statues are returned to their original spots. **Hacienda San Jose** is located in Mérida, the capital of Yucatán, which means guests are in the center of the action.

THE LUXURY COLLECTION HOTEL DIRECTORY

DISCOVER MORE AT THELUXURYCOLLECTION.COM

AFRICA

ETHIOPIA
SHERATON ADDIS

Sits on a hilltop overlooking the city, safely nestled between the National Palace and the prime minister's residence.

Taitu St, Addis Ababa 1000
telephone 251 11 517 1717

SEYCHELLES
NORTH ISLAND

Experience your own private island in the Seychelles. Situated thirty kilometers north of Mahé, North Island offers complete privacy for the ultimate romantic retreat or exclusive family escape.

Ile du Nord, North Island
telephone 248 4 293 100

ASIA

CHINA
THE AZURE QIANTANG

The mythic Qiantang River sets the scene at the Azure Qiantang, where the concierge recommends a private sculling boat trip to explore an ancient pilgrimage route and the largest tidal bore in the world.

39 East Wangjiang Road
Shangcheng District
Hangzhou, Zhejiang 310008
telephone 86 571 2823 7777

CHINA
THE CASTLE HOTEL

Overlooking vibrant Xinghai Bay, The Castle Hotel boasts three sophisticated restaurants, a lounge and a spa. Its grand ballrooms serve as settings for truly memorable occasions.

600 Binhai West Road
Shahekou District
Dalian, Liaoning 116023
telephone 86 411 8656 0000

CHINA
THE HONGTA HOTEL

Located in Pudong's business center, close to the Bund and Century Park, The Hongta Hotel embraces a vibrant mix of culture and luxury. Explore the best of what Shanghai has to offer, from attractions to eateries.

889 Dong Fang Road, Pudong District
Shanghai 200122
telephone 86 21 5050 4567

CHINA
MEIXI LAKE HOTEL

Elegant accommodations and modern facilities blend into an urban oasis of serene lake views, captivating culture and layered history.

1177 Huanhu Road, Yuelu District
Changsha, Hunan 410006
telephone 86 731 8869 8888

CHINA
NA LOTUS HOTEL

Na Lotus Hotel invites travelers to explore the distinctive charm of Nanning and guides guests on transformative journeys that touch their spirits and enrich their lives.

Tower A, Logan Century
8 Zhongjian Road
Qingxiu District, Nanning
telephone 86 771 255 8888

INDIA
ITC GARDENIA

Set in the commercial heart of Bengaluru, ITC Gardenia is a verdant sanctuary exuding natural sophistication and elegance. With its ambience of nature combined with luxury, warm hospitality and superlative facilities, ITC Gardenia lives the "Responsible Luxury" promise and is a tribute to the Garden City.

1 Residency Road
Bengaluru 560025
telephone 91 80 2211 9898

INDIA
ITC GRAND BHARAT

The resort's 300 acres encompass elaborate conference facilities and recreation and wellness services, and offer top-notch culinary experiences. Envisioned as a supreme leisure getaway destination, the hotel is situated in an idyllic expanse, just outside Delhi, surrounded by the majestic Aravalli range and dotted with pristine lakes.

P.O. Hasanpur Tauru
Mewat District, Gurgaon 122105
telephone 91 1267 285 500

INDIA
ITC GRAND CENTRAL

Inspired by Victorian architecture of Old Bombay, this landmark LEED® Platinum–certified hotel is situated in the business and recreational center of Parel. The hotel offers breathtaking views of the city, award-winning cuisine, elegantly appointed rooms and suites, signature wellness experiences and more.

287, Dr Babasaheb Ambedkar Road, Parel,
Mumbai, Maharashtra, 400012
telephone 91 22 2410 1010

INDIA
ITC GRAND CHOLA

In its grandeur and majesty, this 600-room masterpiece is an inspired rendition of the vision of South India's great masters. With the hotel's perfect synergy of history, refined opulence and unparalleled service, guests can enjoy an exceptional indigenous luxury experience.

63 Mount Road, Guindy, Chennai
Tamil Nadu 600032
telephone 91 44 2220 0000

INDIA
ITC GRAND GOA

Nestled in serene South Goa, amid a lush 45 acres of landscaped gardens, swaying coconut palms and shimmering lagoons, the ITC Grand Goa Resort & Spa, with direct access to the pristine Arossim Beach, provides all the ingredients for an invigorating or intimate, relaxed getaway.

Arossim Beach, Cansaulim
South Goa 403712
telephone 91 832 272 1234

INDIA
ITC KAKATIYA

Discover opulence in the heart of Hyderabad's commercial district, as authentic Kakatiya décor unites with singular views of Lake Hussain Sagar. This hotel is a true homage to the legendary Kakatiya Dynasty.

6-3-1187 Begumpet, Hyderabad
Telangana 500016
telephone 91 40 2340 0132

INDIA
ITC KOHENUR

Located in the heart of Hyderabad's new business district and overlooking the picturesque Durgam Lake, ITC Kohenur is an ode to those rare and priceless experiences and creations we proudly call our own.

Plot No. 5 Survey No. 83/1
Hyderabad Knowledge City
Madhapur, Hyderabad 500081
telephone 91 40 6766 0101

INDIA
ITC MARATHA

Elegance and history merge to reveal the city's rich culture. Saluting the legacy of the Grand Marathas, this hotel presents a range of cuisines, accommodations and recreational options with the warmth of Indian hospitality for an unmistakably majestic experience.

Sahar Airport Road, near International Airport
Andheri (East), Mumbai 400099
telephone 91 22 2830 3030

INDIA
ITC MAURYA

Situated in the diplomatic enclave of New Delhi, with more than 400 luxurious rooms and suites, world-renowned cuisine and a deep understanding of the needs of the global traveler, this hotel is the preferred accommodation for heads of state and global statesmen of business.

Sardar Patel Marg, Akhaura Block,
Diplomatic Enclave
Chanakyapuri, New Delhi, Delhi 110021
telephone 91 11 2611 2233

INDIA
ITC MUGHAL

Sprawled over 23 acres of lush gardens and water features near the magnificent Taj Mahal, this hotel is a tribute to the Mughal era. ITC Mughal boasts the country's largest and most luxurious spa (Kaya Kalp–the Royal Spa), along with a range of fine-dining options.

Taj Ganj, Agra
Uttar Pradesh 282001
telephone 91 562 402 1700

INDIA
ITC RAJPUTANA

Centrally located, ITC Rajputana is the perfect blend of Rajasthani architecture and Rajput hospitality. The *haveli-*inspired architecture and regal design echo the city's history, while the balconies from the guest rooms face an intricate network of internal courtyards.

Palace Road
Jaipur 302006
telephone 91 141 405 1600

INDIA
ITC ROYAL BENGAL

Located on the cusp of the business district and the city, ITC Royal Bengal is an ode to the region's cultural heritage and lineage. This monumental, magnificent edifice towers over Kolkata's skyline and blends fine European and indigenous architecture with contemporary design.

1, JBS Haldane Avenue, Tangra, Kolkata,
West Bengal 700046, India
telephone 91 33 4446 4646

INDIA
ITC SONAR

Celebrating the Golden Era of Bengal, ITC Sonar is a verdant oasis just minutes from the heart of Kolkata. Garden houses, large green spaces and water features reminiscent of the Baghbaris create a captivating setting, while a well-appointed spa provides modern-day comforts in the City of Joy.

JBS Haldane Avenue (opposite Science City), Kolkata 700046
telephone 91 33 2345 4545

INDIA
ITC WINDSOR

Located in the heart of Bengaluru, ITC Windsor has access to business parks and tourist attractions, making it an ideal choice for leisure and business travelers. It is also the first hotel in the world to achieve LEED Zero Carbon certification.

Windsor Square, 25, Golf Course Road
Bengaluru 560052
telephone 91 80 2226 9898

INDONESIA
THE LAGUNA

Nestled on Bali's finest white-sand beach, overlooking the majestic Indian Ocean and expansive, swimmable lagoons, The Laguna is situated perfectly in the enchanting Nusa Dua enclave.

Kawasan Pariwisata Nusa Dua Lot N2
Nusa Dua, Bali 80363
telephone 62 361 771327

JAPAN
HOTEL THE MITSUI KYOTO

The hotel is in the heart of Kyoto, adjacent to Nijo-jo Castle on the site of the Kyoto home of the Kitake, the executive branch of the Mitsui family–a property the family maintained for over 250 years. The tranquility and storied history of the location are reflected in each of the guest rooms.

Aburano-Koji St. Nijo-Sagaru, 284
Nijoaburanokoji-Cho, Nakagyo Ward,
Kyoto 604-0051, Japan
telephone 81 75 468 3100

JAPAN
IRAPH SUI

Located on Irabu Island, just southwest of the island of Okinawa, the hotel is surrounded by primeval forests, the sea and the rich culture of Miyakojima, Okinawa and Irabu Island.

818-5 Irabu Irabu-nagasokobaru
Miyakojima-city 905-0503
telephone 81 980 74 5511

JAPAN
THE PRINCE GALLERY TOKYO KIOICHO

Near businesses and landmarks in Tokyo's most dignified neighborhood, this hotel welcomes guests with innovative interiors and upscale guest rooms.

1-2 Kioi-cho Chiyoda-ku
Tokyo 102-8585
telephone 81 3 3234 1111

JAPAN
SUIRAN

This hotel offers authentic Japanese experiences within a historic Kyoto community—a peaceful riverfront haven steps from the Tenryu-ji World Heritage site.

12 Susukinobaba-cho, Saga-Tenryuji
Ukyo-ku, Kyoto
telephone 81 75 872 0101

SOUTH KOREA
JOSUN PALACE

A world-class luxury hotel presented by the Josun Hotel & Resort brand. Our timeless hotel combines a century of hospitality with modernistic sentiments to offer guests a singular, storied experience in South Korea's capital.

Teheran-ro, 231 Gangnam-gu, Seoul,
South Korea
telephone 82 2 727 7200

THAILAND
THE ATHENEE HOTEL

Located on the grounds of Kandhavas Palace, this iconic hotel is renowned as one of the most prestigious addresses in central Bangkok.

61 Wireless Road (Witthayu)
Lumpini, Pathumwan
Bangkok 10330
telephone 66 26 508 800

THAILAND
THE NAKA ISLAND

With endless views of Phang Nga Bay and the Phuket landscape, this five-star island retreat is private, romantic and idyllic.

32 Moo 5, Tambol Paklok
Amphur Thalang, Naka Yai Island
Phuket 83110
telephone 66 76 371 400

THAILAND
SHERATON GRANDE SUKHUMVIT

This hotel features guest rooms that pay homage to local culture, from exotic teakwood to shimmering Thai silks. Hotel guests can find respite in the heart of Bangkok at The Sala, a tropical garden surrounding a free-form pool.

250 Sukhumvit Road
Bangkok 10110
telephone 66 2 649 8888

THAILAND
VANA BELLE

Overlooking the breathtaking Gulf of Siam, Vana Belle offers an enchanting getaway and memorable experiences in one of Thailand's most beautiful locations.

9/99 Moo 3, Chaweng Noi Beach, Surat Thani
Koh Samui 84320
telephone 66 77 915 555

AUSTRALIA

AUSTRALIA
THE TASMAN

Journey to the 1800s with a stay at this architecturally stunning and historically rich hotel in the heart of Tasmania's capital.

12 Murray St, Hobart TAS 7000, Australia
telephone 61 3 6240 6000

EUROPE

ARMENIA
THE ALEXANDER

The mixture of old and new is exemplified by The Alexander, which boasts a prestigious central location one block from Republic Square.

3/4 Abovyan Street
Yerevan 0001
telephone 374 1 120 6000

AUSTRIA
HOTEL BRISTOL

Located near the Vienna State Opera in the heart of the city, this luxury hotel provides an oasis from the bustle of a busy metropolis. The concierge recommends visiting the elegant Winter Palace of Prince Eugene of Savoy, right in the city center.

Kaerntner Ring 1, Vienna 1010
telephone 43 1 515 160

AUSTRIA
HOTEL GOLDENER HIRSCH

Sip the signature Susanne cocktail, eat the famous Rigo Jancsi dessert and live in luxury while attending nearby summer festivals in Salzburg.

Getreidegasse 37
Salzburg 5020
telephone 43 6 628 0840

AUSTRIA
HOTEL IMPERIAL

Experience the essence of Vienna at this elegant and beautiful hotel, and delight in the Viennese coffee tradition by enjoying a cup of coffee and a slice of the renowned Imperial Torte.

Kaerntner Ring 16
Vienna, 1015
telephone 43 1 501 100

CYPRUS
PARKLANE

Nestled on the southern coastal strip of Cyprus, surrounded by palm trees and snuggled by the Mediterranean Sea, the resort is the ideal hideaway for couples, families, groups of friends or single travelers seeking a memorable escape.

11 Giannou Kranidioti Street
Limassol 4534
telephone 357 2586 2000

CZECH REPUBLIC
HOTEL AUGUSTINE

Located in a thirteenth-century Augustinian monastery, the hotel boasts impeccable service and design inspired by early-twentieth-century Czech cubism.

Letenská 12/33
Prague 118 00
telephone 420 2 6611 2233

FRANCE
HÔTEL DE BERRI

Located in the fashionable eighth arrondissement, the hotel is distinguished by an expansive private park and an extraordinary art collection.

18-22 Rue de Berri
Paris 75008
telephone 33 1 76 53 77 70

FRANCE
PRINCE DE GALLES

Just steps away from the Champs-Élysées, this Art Deco hotel, a mosaic of discreet Parisian elegance, is located in the heart of the city and offers exceptional hospitality and superb Japanese cuisine by Michelin-starred chef Akira Back.

33 Avenue George V
Paris 75008
telephone 33 1 53 237777

GREECE
BLUE PALACE ELOUNDA

Blue Palace is a place where luxury meets wild beauty and unrivaled island style. Venture beyond the ordinary with life-lasting authentic adventures, embracing history and local culture and accommodations that offer the feeling of a truer, more timeless Greece.

Elounda, Crete 72053
telephone 30 284 106 5500

GREECE
COSME

Set in the soulful, whitewashed village of Naoussa—the jewel of Paros—with the clear-blue Aegean at its feet, Cosme embraces the energy of the sea and reciprocates the joyful pulse of the town.

Naoussa, Paros, 844 01
telephone 30 228 444 0000

GREECE
DOMES MIRAMARE

Renovated with refined natural materials and decorated with contemporary art pieces, Domes Miramare Corfu is a legendary amalgamation of opulent style and design, set in an authentic Mediterranean landscape.

Miramare Beach Moraitika
Corfu 49084
telephone 30 2661 440500

GREECE
DOMES ZEEN CHANIA

A head-turning harbor of slow living, centered around the Greek concept of *ef zeen* (or the art of living well), Domes Zeen is a beachfront cove for contemplation, reconnection, exploration and making lifelong memories.

Apteron Road Parigoria, Kon/nou
Paleologou, Chania 731 00
telephone 30 2821 607000

GREECE
HOTEL GRANDE BRETAGNE

With unsurpassed views of the Acropolis and Parthenon, Constitution Square and Lycabettus Hill, this hotel offers unrivaled access to Athens's mythical history.

1 Vasileos Georgiou A' str.
Syntagma Square, Athens 10564
telephone 30 210 333 0000

GREECE
KING GEORGE

Just two kilometers from the Acropolis, this hotel has welcomed many celebrities and hosted many events in its 350-square-meter penthouse suite under the illuminated sky.

Vas Georgiou A' Street 3
Athens 10564
telephone 30 210 322 2210

GREECE
MYSTIQUE

Carved into the rugged caldera cliffs of the island of Santorini, Mystique overlooks the midnight-blue waters of the Aegean Sea.

Oia, Santorini 84702
telephone 30 228 607 1114

GREECE
THE ROMANOS

Guests can indulge in one of Anazoe Spa's signature treatments, experience tennis at Europe's first Mouratoglou Tennis Center and scuba-dive with Navarino Sea—all experiences that can be arranged by the concierge.

Navarino Dunes, Costa Navarino
Messinia 24001
telephone 30 272 309 6000

GREECE
SANTA MARINA

The getaway you dream of all year round and the place you truly long for. Where you feel the sun on your back, the water gently lapping on your feet and the tantalizing prospect of a fun night ahead. When you're with us, you feel inspired and invigorated by the sense of belonging.

Ornos Bay
Mykonos, South Aegean 84600
telephone 30 228 902 3220

GREECE
VEDEMA RESORT

Tucked away within the medieval village of Megalochori, the enchanting Vedema has evolved from a 400-year-old wine cellar into an authentic Cycladic retreat.

Megalochori, Santorini 84700
telephone 30 228 608 1796

HUNGARY
MATILD PALACE

Matild Palace welcomes guests with a distinctive ambience representative of its Hungarian heritage, which runs beautifully through its core and is unmistakable from the moment you step through the front door.

Budapest, Váci u 36, 1056
telephone 36 1 550 5000

ISRAEL
THE JAFFA

Residing within Tel Aviv, the old city of Jaffa is a lifestyle destination renowned for its historic port, flea market and culinary scene.

2 Louis Pasteur Street
Tel Aviv-Jaffa 6803602
telephone 972 3504 2000

Following pages: (*left*) Traditional performance in Jaipur, India. (*right*)
Hot-air-balloon ride over the breathtaking landscape of Jordan.

ITALY
EXCELSIOR HOTEL GALLIA

The hotel is located in the heart of Milan, Italy's ever-evolving capital of fashion, design and gastronomy. Its strategic location acts as entryway to Italy's most captivating destinations, whether day-tripping to Lake Como or further afield to Florence, Rome and Venice.

Piazza Duca D'Aosta 9
Milan 20124
telephone 39 02 67851

ITALY
FALISIA RESORT

A wellness paradise, embracing a breathtaking sea view. Indulge in delectable gourmet cuisine and indelible experiences in and along the Gulf of Trieste.

Str. Portopiccolo 231/M
Località Sistiana, Duino Aurisina 34011
telephone 39 040 997 4444

ITALY
THE GRITTI PALACE

Occupying a prestigious setting on the Grand Canal, The Gritti Palace is where history and culture meet with renewed Venetian style. A leisurely short stroll from Piazza San Marco, the imposing palazzo offers rare views of Santa Maria della Salute.

Campo Santa Maria del Giglio 2467
Venice 30124
telephone 39 041 794611

ITALY
HOTEL CALA DI VOLPE

Stretching out over the bay like a timeless village and seemingly sculpted by the wind, Hotel Cala di Volpe embodies a glamorous elegance immersed between the colors and scents of nature and sea. It is a natural set for exclusive events, such as concerts with gala dinners.

Costa Smeralda, Porto Cervo 07020
telephone 39 0789 976111

ITALY
HOTEL PITRIZZA

Like a precious gem located in the midst of rocks and flowers, made up of romantic rooms and exquisite private villas, Hotel Pitrizza is an unforgettable getaway where intimacy and privacy are guaranteed.

Costa Smeralda, Porto Cervo 07020
telephone 39 0789 930111

ITALY
HOTEL ROMAZZINO

Between emerald waters and verdant scented gardens lies the whitewashed Hotel Romazzino, gently resting on a lengthy beach of the finest sand. It is the epitome of unrivaled indulgent relaxation, perfect for vacationers who want to have a full beach resort experience.

Costa Smeralda, Porto Cervo 07020
telephone 39 0789 977111

POLAND
HOTEL BRISTOL

This hotel, a recognized landmark since 1901, lies right on the Royal Route, a road that leads through the historic district of the city and is dotted with examples of stunning architecture.

Krakowskie Przedmiescie 42/44
Warsaw 00-325
telephone 48 22 551 1000

PORTUGAL
PINE CLIFFS RESORT

Enjoy breathtaking views of the surroundings, warm weather year-round and the beautiful golf course, including its famed and most challenging hole, Devil's Parlour, at this luxury hotel.

Praia Da Falésia, Pinhal do Concelho
Albufeira 8200-593
telephone 351 289 500100

SLOVAKIA
GRAND HOTEL RIVER PARK

The Slovakian capital's leading hotel is distinguished by its accessibility, sleek décor, spacious accommodations and expansive spa.

Dvorakovo Nabrezie 6
Bratislava 81102
telephone 421 2 32238 222

SPAIN
CASTILLO HOTEL SON VIDA

An adults-only haven, open all-year long, with fully renovated rooms and suites, a first-class spa, swimming pools and luxurious dining venues, surrounded by four excellent golf courses.

C/Raixa 2, Urbanizacion Son Vida
Palma de Mallorca 07013
telephone 34 971 493493

SPAIN
HOTEL ALFONSO XIII

This hotel is one of the most monumental landmarks in Seville, embodying the city's layered history, architecture and authentic cuisine in a luxurious atmosphere.

San Fernando 2
Seville 41004
telephone 34 95 491 7000

SPAIN
HOTEL MARIA CRISTINA

Indulge in a mouthwatering local culinary experience when visiting this charming hotel, near the Michelin-starred restaurants of San Sebastián.

Paseo Republica Argentina 4
San Sebastián 20004
telephone 34 943 437600

SPAIN
HOTEL MARQUÉS DE RISCAL

Frank Gehry's design houses a collection of wines that any wine lover will enjoy. The hotel offers guided cultural tours to truly take in the surrounding area.

Calle Torrea 1
Elciego 01340
telephone 34 945 180880

SPAIN
SANTO MAURO

With its French-influenced design and architecture, the hotel consists of three buildings set in the most sophisticated private garden in Madrid, with fountains and terraces shaded by ancient chestnut trees.

Calle de Zurbano, 36, Madrid
telephone 34 913 19 69 00

SWITZERLAND
HOTEL PRESIDENT WILSON

Steps away from Geneva's lakefront, this luxury hotel allows one to explore such local attractions as the Jet d'Eau, the Flower Clock and St. Peter's Cathedral.

47, Quai Wilson
Geneva 1211
telephone 41 22 906 6666

TURKEY
CARESSE BODRUM

The iconic Barbarossa Bodrum restaurant (with its stunning seafood), panoramic views of Karaada, Asian fusion cuisine in the world-famous Buddha Bar Beach (with legendary DJ performances), and more await guests at Caresse Bodrum.

Adnan Menderes caddesi No. 89
Asarlik Mevkii PK 225
Bodrum
telephone 90 252 311 3636

TURKEY
LUGAL

Immerse yourself in local culture, as original paintings by local artists are found throughout this luxury hotel.

Noktali Sokak No. 1, 'Kavaklidere
Ankara 06700
telephone 90 312 457 6050

TURKEY
REGES

Bringing Cesme to life in an unprecedented and dynamic fashion, Reges is where exceptional location, thoughtful design and bespoke service combine to infuse a deep sense of calm and lasting experience.

Boyalik Mahallesi 3198/1, Sokak No. 5/2
Cesme, Izmir 35930
telephone 90 232 292 0000

UNITED KINGDOM
THE LANGLEY

Sitting in the former hunting lodge of the third Duke of Marlborough, this grand country manor rests amid 150 acres of formal gardens and parklands, offering an escape where time slows and natural beauty abounds.

Avenue Drive, Uxbridge Road
Iver, England, SL3 6DU
telephone 44 20 7236 3636

UNITED KINGDOM
THE PARK TOWER KNIGHTSBRIDGE

While at this hotel, guests can visit the vibrant Serpentine Gallery and the world-renowned Royal Albert Hall, enjoy spectacular views across Hyde Park and the London skyline from spacious suites, and take advantage of the bespoke butler service.

101 Knightsbridge
London, England SW1X 7RN
telephone 44 207 235 8050

UNITED KINGDOM
THE WELLESLEY KNIGHTSBRIDGE

Boutique and grand elements exist harmoniously in this Knightsbridge hotel near London's best hidden gems, fabled parks, renowned shopping and historic landmarks.

11 Knightsbridge
London, England SW1X 7LY
telephone 44 20 7235 3535

LATIN AMERICA

ARGENTINA
PARK TOWER

Unparalleled service, an in-hotel shopping arcade and a heart-of-the-city location set this luxury hotel apart.

Avenida Leandro N. Alem 1193
Buenos Aires 1001
telephone 54 11 4318 9100

DOMINICAN REPUBLIC
THE OCEAN CLUB

Experience bliss in a modern and sophisticated setting, with a lush tropical landscape, a deep-blue ocean and soft golden sand.

Playa Imbert, Puerto Plata
telephone 1 877 248 9850

DOMINICAN REPUBLIC
SANCTUARY CAP CANA

Sanctuary Cap Cana provides guests with an expansive sense of possibility: extraordinary gastronomical options, five specialty restaurants, seven lounges and preferred access to Sanctuary Town, a small village with stylish dining and entertainment.

Boulevard Zona Hotelera
Punta Cana, 23302
telephone 1 809 562 9191

MEXICO
HACIENDA PUERTA CAMPECHE

This hotel is a collection of restored seventeenth-century historic houses, allowing one to enjoy the beauty of a Mexican hacienda with excellent personal service.

Calle 59, No. 71 por 16 & 18
Campeche, Campeche 24000
telephone 52 981 816 7508

MEXICO
HACIENDA SAN JOSE

An authentic Mayan experience awaits in the Mayan Villas, while luxury tastes can be indulged with massages at the spa.

KM 30 Carretera Tixkokob-Tekanto
Tixkokob, Yucatán 97470
telephone 52 999 924 1333

MEXICO
HACIENDA SANTA ROSA

Bird watching, Mayan lessons, cocktail demonstrations and tours of the botanical garden are all offered at this luxury hotel.

Carretera Mérida Campeche
Desviación Maxcanú, Santa Rosa, 97800
telephone 52 999 923 1923

MEXICO
HACIENDA TEMOZÓN

Explore the unique spa, where one can experience individual spa treatments in a beautifully preserved cavern.

KM 182 Carretera Merida-Uxmal
Temozon Sur, Yucatán 97825
telephone 52 999 923 8089

MEXICO
HACIENDA UAYAMON

Bulbous pegs set into stone walls can be found throughout this hotel, allowing guests to hang woven cotton hammocks and sleep in the Mayan style.

KM 20 Carretera, Uayamon-China-Edzná
Uayamon
telephone 52 981 813 0530

MEXICO
LAS ALCOBAS

Refined hospitality with an intimate environment at the most exclusive address, in the heart of Polanco in Mexico City. Known for its elegant architectural features and residential feel, Las Alcobas is an unforgettable experience that delights connoisseurs.

Ave. Presidente Masaryk 390
Ciudad de México, 11560
telephone 52 55 3300 3900

MEXICO
SOLAZ

Discover Solaz's striking architecture, which seamlessly blends with the unique landscape where the desert meets the sea.

KM 18.5 Carretera Transpeninsular CSL-SJC
Cabo Real, San Jose del Cabo
Baja California Sur 23405
telephone 52 624 144 0500

PANAMA
THE SANTA MARIA

In the heart of Panama, this contemporary hotel invites guests to uncover the cobblestone streets of Panama Viejo and modern marvels like Frank Gehry's Biomuseo.

Calle 125 Este, Urbanizacion Llano Bonito
Panama City
telephone 507 304 5555

PERU
PALACIO DEL INKA

Located in the historic center of Cusco, this hotel dates back almost five centuries and offers easy access to museums, markets and restaurants. Its property also boasts a relaxing therapy pool.

Plazoleta Santo Domingo 259
Cusco
telephone 51 84 231 961

PERU
HOTEL PARACAS

A bottle of local pisco, windsurfing lessons and private-jet flights over the Nazca Lines are all offered at this luxury hotel. The concierge suggests traveling back in time with a visit to the intriguing archaeological site Tambo Colorado.

Av. Paracas S/N
Paracas
telephone 51 56 581 333

PERU
TAMBO DEL INKA

Enjoy views of the Vilcanota River while swimming in the hotel pool. Take a guided trip to the Valle Sagrado, and escape to Machu Picchu from the hotel's private train station.

Avenida Ferrocarril S/N
Sacred Valley, Urubamba
telephone 51 84 581 777

MIDDLE EAST

JORDAN
AL MANARA

Jordan's rich culture is reflected in the traditional architecture, sumptuous décor and magnificent surroundings of this seaside escape.

Al-Hashemi Street
Aqaba 1968
telephone 962 3 202 1010

QATAR
AL MESSILA

Set within an urban oasis of lush gardens, the resort boasts luxurious rooms, suites and villas, providing comfort and privacy. Enjoy eight restaurants and lounges, a grand outdoor pool and the region's largest spa, which revives you through the healing power of water.

Zone 36, Street 827, Building 21, Doha
telephone 974 4445 0000

SAUDI ARABIA
ASSILA

The epitome of understated luxury and exclusivity, Assila is a celebration of Jeddah's progress. A modern masterpiece that artfully blends traditional Arabian hospitality with contemporary sophistication.

Prince Mohammed Bin Abdulaziz St,
Al Andalus, Jeddah 23326
telephone 966 12 231 9800

UNITED ARAB EMIRATES
AJMAN SARAY

Situated along the Arabian Gulf, just minutes from Dubai, this resort overlooks endless expanses of pristine sand and shimmering sea.

Sheikh Humaid Bin Rashid Al Nuaimi Street
Ajman 8833
telephone 971 6 714 2222

UNITED ARAB EMIRATES
AL MAHA

With Arabian wildlife such as the oryx and gazelle as star attractions, the panoramic views of the conservation reserve can be seen from the temperature-controlled infinity pools or sundeck areas of all suites.

Dubai Desert Conservation Reserve
Dubai-Al Ain Road, Dubai 118887
telephone 971 4 832 9900

UNITED ARAB EMIRATES
AL WATHBA

Deep within the desert landscape lies Al Wathba, an intimate retreat suffused with natural beauty and tranquility.

Al Wathba South
P.O. Box 56620, Abu Dhabi
telephone 971 02 204 4444

UNITED ARAB EMIRATES
GROSVENOR HOUSE

This lifestyle destination, located in the cosmopolitan area of Dubai Marina, offers access to fantastic restaurants, including the hotel's world-famous Buddha-Bar.

Al Emreef Street
P.O. Box 118500
Dubai
telephone 971 4 399 8888

NORTH AMERICA

UNITED STATES
THE BALLANTYNE

Located in south Charlotte overlooking a beautiful community park, this Southern beauty features signature whiskey cocktails, formal tea service, luxurious lodging and alluring spa treatments.

10000 Ballantyne Commons Parkway
Charlotte, North Carolina 28277
telephone 1 704 248 4000

UNITED STATES
THE CANYON SUITES AT THE PHOENICIAN

Discover the Valley of the Sun's only Forbes Five Star, AAA Five Diamond resort-within-a-resort. Enjoy a complimentary daily artisan breakfast, chauffeured resort and local transportation, a private infinity pool and exclusive events and experiences.

6000 East Camelback Road
Scottsdale, Arizona 85251
telephone 1 480 941 8200

UNITED STATES
HOTEL CLIO

Located in Denver's chic shopping district of Cherry Creek North, Hotel Clio is for travelers seeking a refined and inspirational stay.

150 Clayton Lane, Denver, Colorado 80206
telephone 1 303 316 2700

UNITED STATES
THE GWEN

This opulent hotel along the Magnificent Mile boasts modern amenities, spacious guest rooms and fine dining in an inviting atmosphere.

521 North Rush Street
Chicago, Illinois 60611
telephone 1 312 645 1500

UNITED STATES
THE HYTHE

The Hythe is your gateway to Vail's most exciting experiences: exclusive alpine excursions, unforgettable culinary offerings and our signature Well & Being Spa. Inspired by the passions of Vail Mountain's legendary founders, The Hythe infuses a convivial "après all day" spirit into every moment.

715 West Lionshead Circle, Vail
Colorado 81657
telephone 1 970 476 4444

UNITED STATES
THE JOSEPH

Authentic in spirit and sophisticated in aesthetic, The Joseph is a hotel with deep local roots and worldly relevance, and invites guests to indulge in an artfully crafted experience of Nashville at its most refined.

401 Korean Veterans Blvd, Nashville,
Tennessee 37203
telephone 1 615 248 1990

UNITED STATES
HOTEL IVY

Of all the destinations to be discovered, few are filled with such surprises as the contemporary yet affable city of Minneapolis. The Hotel Ivy is the key to unlocking your guide to indigenous, exceptional and collectible experiences.

201 South Eleventh Street
Minneapolis, Minnesota 55403
telephone 1 612 746 4600

UNITED STATES
THE LIBERTY

Guests of this beautiful hotel are exposed to the best of Boston, from sweeping views of the skyline to complimentary Liberty-branded bicycles for riding around town. The iconic Freedom Trail is a must for any history buff.

215 Charles Street
Boston, Massachusetts 02114
telephone 1 617 224 4000

UNITED STATES
THE NINES

Step into the historic Meier and Frank department store turned Portland's finest hotel, with an art-forward aura and unique personalized service.

525 SW Morrison Street
Portland, Oregon 97204
telephone 1 503 222 9996

UNITED STATES
PALACE HOTEL

Originally built in 1875, the Palace is San Francisco's first luxury hotel. A historic landmark, the award-winning Palace is home to treasures like The Garden Court, the Pied Piper of Hamelin painting and Landmark 18 museum.

2 New Montgomery Street
San Francisco, California 94105
telephone 1 415 512 1111

UNITED STATES
PERRY LANE HOTEL

Equidistant from River Street and Forsyth Park, this vibrant hotel welcomes guests with worldly elegance and Southern hospitality.

256 East Perry Street
Savannah, Georgia 31401
telephone 1 912 415 9000

UNITED STATES
THE PHOENICIAN

Nestled at the base of Camelback Mountain, this awe-inspiring Sonoran Desert destination offers a variety of signature amenities, including exceptional golf, multi-tiered pools, a state-of-the-art athletic club and a Forbes Five Star spa.

6000 East Camelback Road
Scottsdale, Arizona 85251
telephone 1 480 941 8200

UNITED STATES
THE ROYAL HAWAIIAN

Offering Hawaiian hospitality since 1927, the iconic "Pink Palace of the Pacific" graces the perfect location on Waikiki Beach. The hotel combines historical legacy with contemporary comfort for the discerning world traveler seeking an idyllic location in paradise.

2259 Kalakaua Avenue
Honolulu, Hawaii 96815
telephone 1 808 923 7311

UNITED STATES
SLS HOTEL
BEVERLY HILLS

This modern luxury property located at the crossroads of Los Angeles and Beverly Hills boasts two rooftop pools with sweeping vistas of the surrounding area, a serene spa, a fanciful speakeasy and two distinctive restaurants.

465 S. La Cienega Boulevard
Los Angeles, California 90048
telephone 1 310 247 0400

UNITED STATES
THE ST. ANTHONY

Since its opening in 1909, The St. Anthony Hotel has been the premier luxury hotel of San Antonio. Now featuring a timeless interior with a contemporary design, our hotel is the place to stay in San Antonio with glamorous guest rooms, unique culinary experiences and world-class service. Overlooking Travis Park, our downtown hotel is centrally located to many San Antonio attractions.

300 East Travis Street
San Antonio, Texas 78205
telephone 1 210 227 4392

UNITED STATES
THE US GRANT

A presidential landmark nestled amid the vibrancy of downtown San Diego's famed Gaslamp Quarter, the hotel weaves its storied history into an oasis of fine art and epicurean innovation.

326 Broadway
San Diego, California 92101
telephone 1 619 232 3121

UNITED STATES
THE WHITLEY

Set amid Buckhead's upscale shopping, dining and nightlife, the hotel extends its signature elegance from its guest rooms to the spa to the ample event space.

3434 Peachtree Road, Northeast
Atlanta, Georgia 30326
telephone 1 404 237 2700

Following pages: A spectacular demonstration on the sands of Koh Samui, Thailand.

PHOTOGRAPHY CREDITS

Back cover (clockwise from top left): © Betsy Newman; © Yogendra Singh/Pexels; © Laurent Philippe/Courtesy of The Romanos; © Federico Tovoli Photo/Alamy Stock Photo; © Marriott International; © China Photos/Getty Images; © Visual China Group/Getty Images; © Marriott International; © Marriott International.

Endpages: © WinWin artlab/Shutterstock.

All images © Marriott International, except: page 6: © Emanuel Tadeu/Pexels; p. 9: © Abraham Pacheco/Pexels; pp. 12–13: © Laura Saffioti/EyeEm/Getty Images; p. 14: (bottom) © Urs Hauenstein/Alamy Stock Photo; p. 15: © Alvaro German Vilela/Dreamstime; p. 16: © Mcmorabad/Dreamstime; p. 17: (top) © Zkruger/Dreamstime, (bottom) © Dennis Cox/Alamy Stock Photo; p. 18: (top) © Michael Tewelde/Xinhua News Agency/Getty Images; p. 20: (top) © Maxwell De Araujo Rodrigues/Dreamstime, (bottom) © Vishal Bhatnagar/NurPhoto/Getty Images; p. 21: (top) © Wiener Philharmoniker/Filip Waldmann, (bottom) © Wolf-Dieter Grabner; pp. 22–23: © Carlos Sánchez Mejía; p. 24: © Lloyd Vas/Dreamstime; p. 25: (top) © Indranil Mukherjee/AFP/Getty Images; pp. 26 (left), 27 (top left): © Scottsdale Arabian Horse Show/Osteen Schatzberg Photography; p. 27: (top right) © Terry Vacha/Alamy Stock Photo; p. 29: (top left) © Luca Dugaro/Unsplash, (top right) © Charlotte Harrison/Unsplash; p. 30: (left) Ben Ford Photography/Courtesy of The Hythe; p. 31: © Shubham Mahitkar/Pexels, (bottom) © Jcfmorata/Dreamstime; p. 32: © Christina Kennedy/Alamy Stock Photo; pp. 34–35: Artwork by Nojoud Alsudairi/Photographed by Canvas and Commissioned by SAC; p. 36: (top) © Sanjay Borra/Alamy Stock Photo, (bottom) © Kosigeethareddy/Dreamstime; p. 37: (top) © Warren Little/Getty Images, (bottom) © Francois Nel/Getty Images; p. 38: (bottom) © Nicholas Gill/Alamy Stock Photo; p. 39: (top) © TPG/Getty Images; pp 40–41: © Yogendra Singh/Pexels; p. 43: all © Kadagan/Shutterstock, except (top left) © James Talalay/Alamy Stock Photo; p. 44: Photography by Suki Zoë/Courtesy of Elora Hardy; p. 46: © Pornsak Na Nakorn/EyeEm/Getty Images; pp. 48–49: © GeorgiaFlash/Alamy Stock Photo; p. 50: (bottom) Courtesy of Salone del Mobile.Milano/Photography by Alessandro Russotti; p. 51: © Noah Seelam/AFP/Getty Images; p. 53: (top left) © Miguel Pereira/Getty Images, (bottom) © Daniel Perez/Getty Images; pp. 56–57: Courtesy of EXPO Chicago/Photo by Justin Barbin Photography; p. 58: (top) © Andre Jenny/Alamy Stock Photo; p. 59: (bottom) © Betsy Newman; p. 61: (top) © Gerry Maceda/Southcreek Global/ZUMA Press, Inc./Alamy Stock Photo; p. 62: (bottom right) © Lee Foster/Alamy Stock Photo; pp. 62–63: © Bromberger Hoover Photography/Getty Images; p. 64: (bottom) © Federico Tovoli Photo/Alamy Stock Photo; p. 68: (top) Photography by Nick Kelsh/Courtesy of Hotel Ivy; p. 69: (bottom) © Glowimages/Getty Images; p. 70: (left) © Andre Wilms/EyeEm/Getty Images; pp. 72 (top), 73 (top): © Elisabetta Loi/REDA&CO/Universal Images Group/Getty Images; pp. 74–75: © Mark Ashbee/Alamy Stock Photo; p. 75: © Philip Sayer/Alamy Stock Photo; p. 77: (top) © Visual China Group/Getty Images, (middle) © Aakahunaa/Dreamstime, (bottom) © Jason Marz/Getty Images; p. 78 (clockwise from top right): © Michal Dolezal/CTK Photo/Alamy Stock Photo, © Frank Chmura/Alamy Stock Photo, © Michal Krumphanzl/CTK Photo/Alamy Stock Photo; p. 79: (bottom) © Christian Goupi/agefotostock/Alamy Stock Photo; p. 80: (top) © Trentham/Dreamstime; p. 82: Photography by Johannes Huebl; p. 83: (top) © David Ducoin/Only France/Alamy Stock Photo; p. 84: (top) Courtesy of Nashville Convention & Visitors Corpo; p. 85: (bottom) © George Vitsaras/Pacific Press/LightRocket/Getty Images; p. 86: (bottom) © Chris Cameron/Alamy Stock Photo; p. 87: (bottom) © Nicolas Randall/Expuesto/Alamy Stock Photo; p. 89: © Tom Hanslien Photography/Alamy Stock Photo; pp. 90–91: © Michel Euler/POOL/AFP/Getty Images; p. 92: (top) © Mohammad Abu Ghosh/Xinhua/Alamy Stock Photo, (bottom) © Ali Jarekji AJ/NL/Reuters/Alamy Stock Photo; p. 93: (bottom) © The Asahi Shimbun/Getty Images; pp. 94–95: © Jumana El-Heloueh/Reuters/Alamy Stock Photo; p. 96: (top) © Chesnot/Getty Images; p. 97: (bottom) © Anna Berkut/Alamy Stock Photo; p. 98 (top & middle), 99: © Ali Balli/Anadolu Agency/Getty Images; p. 100: © Seksak Kerdkanno/Alamy Stock Photo; p. 101: (top) © Helen H. Richardson/*The Denver Post*/Getty Images; p. 102: © Simon Reddy/Alamy Stock Photo; p. 104: (top) © Laurent Philippe/Courtesy of The Romanos, (bottom) © Wim Vandekeybus/Courtesy of The Romanos; p. 105: (left) © Amit Geron, (right) © Itzik Biran; p. 106: (bottom) © Daniel Knighton/Getty Images; p. 107: (bottom) © Martin Siepmann/imageBROKER/Alamy Stock Photo; p. 108: © Sergione Infuso/Corbis/Getty Images; p. 111: (bottom) © Santa Marina, a Luxury Collection Resort, Mykonos; p. 116: (top) © Kobby Dagan/Dreamstime, (bottom) © Snehal Jeevan Pailkar/Dreamstime; p. 117: (top) © Jorge Reyes/EPA-EFE/Shutterstock; p. 118: © Pan Yulong/Xinhua/Alamy Stock Photo; p. 120: © Javier Pardina/Stocksy; pp. 123, 163: © Nick Harvey/Shutterstock; p. 124: (bottom left) © Kacper Pempel/Reuters/Alamy Stock Photo; p. 125: (bottom) © Tomasz Prazmowski/PAP/Alamy Stock Photo; pp. 126–127: © Rudra Narayan Mitra/Dreamstime; p. 128: (bottom) © EndlessJune/Getty Images; p. 129: (top) © Imaginechina Limited/Alamy Stock Photo, (bottom left) © China Photos/Getty Images; p. 133: (top) © Ed Jones/AFP/Getty Images, (middle left) © Jung Yeon-Je/AFP/Getty Images; p. 134: (top) © Andrea Raffin/Alamy Stock Photo; p. 135: (top) © Keith Mundy/Alamy Stock Photo, (bottom) © James Sturcke/Alamy Stock Photo; p. 136: © Pernille Sandberg; p. 137: (top) © Agave Photo Studio/Shutterstock; pp. 138–139: © Anirudh/Unsplash; p. 141: (bottom) © Volker Preusser/Alamy Stock Photo; p. 142: (top) Photography by Mert Jones/Courtesy of Taste of Charlotte; p. 143: (full page) © Miyako Mainichi Shimbun; p. 144: (top) © Bernardo Galmarini/Alamy Stock Photo; p. 145: (top) © Geoff L. Johnson; pp. 146–147: © Loeskieboom/Dreamstime; p. 148: (bottom) © Tim Clayton/Corbis/Getty Images; p. 149: (full page) © Wangyf1983/Dreamstime, (bottom) © Mohd Zakir/*Hindustan Times*/Getty Images; p. 150: (top) © imageBROKER/Shutterstock; p. 152: (top) © Ali Sulima/Dreamstime; p. 153: (top right) © Arijit Sen/*Hindustan Times*/Getty Images, (bottom left) © Raj Singh/Alamy Stock Photo; p. 154: (bottom) © Siiixth/Dreamstime; p. 155: (top) © Vincent Thian/AP/Shutterstock, (middle) © John S Lander/LightRocket/Getty Images, (bottom) © Varuth Pongsapipatt/SOPA Images/LightRocket/Getty Images; pp. 156 (top), 157 (top & middle): © Nacho Urquiza/Courtesy of Las Alcobas; pp. 160–161: Photography by Alastair Bett/Courtesy of The Tasman; p. 162: (top right & bottom) Photography by Pedro Braulio/Courtesy of Sanctuary Cap Cana; p. 164: (left) © AFP/Getty Images; pp. 164–165: © Dominique Berbain/Gamma-Rapho/Getty Images; pp. 166–167: © Gabriel Bouys/AFP/Getty Images; p. 168: (top) © Helen Boast/Getty Images; p. 169: (top) © Genève Tourisme, (bottom) © Alistair Scott/Alamy Stock Photo; pp. 170–171: © Leoh Campos.

DESIGN CREDITS

Pages 14, 68: (border pattern) © janniwet/Shutterstock; pp. 16, 135: (flower illustration) © solarbird/Shutterstock; p. 17: (yellow background) © Mona Eendra/Unsplash; p. 18, 152: (background texture) © Mitchell Luo/Pexels; pp. 20, 162: (brush strokes) © Victorstock/Shutterstock; pp. 26, 37, 38, 80, 128, 130–131, 153: (background texture) © Volodymyr Sanych/Shutterstock; p. 27: (glitter background) © woodpencil/Shutterstock; pp. 28, 64, 122: (border pattern) © Alesia Kozik/Pexels; p. 30: (background texture) © Fabrizio Conti/Unsplash; pp. 34–35: (border pattern) © Koushik Chowdavarapu/Unsplash; pp. 36, 110: (brush strokes) © Anassia Art/Shutterstock; pp. 44, 82, 136, 163: (background texture) © Only background/Shutterstock; pp. 51, 166–167: (border pattern) © Romeo Mike/Pexels; pp. 52, 58, 79, 86, 93, 121: (purple watercolor) © Sonya92/Shutterstock; p. 53: (background pattern) © Carol La Rosa/Shutterstock; p. 55: (text background) © pics five/Shutterstock; pp. 60, 65, 117, 120, 151: (blue watercolor) © Mamuka Gotsiridze/Shutterstock; pp. 62–63: (border pattern) © Xinzheng/Getty Images; pp. 71, 107: (background texture) © mouu007/Shutterstock; pp. 76–77: (border pattern) © charnsitr/Shutterstock; p. 77: (photo frame) © Hamid Ahadi/Shutterstock; pp. 78, 108, 120–121, 129, 168, 170: (background texture) © Olga Thelavart/Unsplash; pp. 78, 129, 153: (paint stroke) © Gumenyuk Dmitriy/Shutterstock; p. 79: (border pattern) © Solen Feyissa/Unsplash; p. 84: (border pattern) © Valentin Salja/Unsplash; pp. 85, 112–113: (border pattern) © Henrik Dønnestad/Unsplash; pp. 88–89: (border pattern) © Josh Hawley/Getty Images; p. 92: (border pattern) © Angèle Kamp/Unsplash; pp. 94–95: (border pattern) © Eva Bronzini/Pexels; p. 97: (border pattern) © helloRuby/Shutterstock; pp. 98, 146–147: (border pattern) © Tamanna Rumee/Unsplash; pp. 103, 141: (background texture) © MM_photos/Shutterstock; pp. 105, 132, 159: (pink paint strokes) © timquo/Shutterstock; p. 106: (border pattern) © Mark Rademaker/Shutterstock; p. 111: (border pattern) © Tim Mossholder/Unsplash; p. 116: (border pattern) © Zakharchuk/Shutterstock; p. 121: (border pattern) © Alice Butenko/Unsplash; pp. 123, 124, 158–159: (background texture) © Paladin12/Shutterstock; p. 134: (border pattern) © MK photograp55/Shutterstock; p. 142: (background texture) © Henry & Co./Unsplash; p. 148: (blue background) © Jason Leung/Unsplash, (text background) © STILLFX/Shutterstock; p. 155: (background texture) © Girl with red hat/Unsplash; p. 156: (border pattern) © Polina Kovaleva/Pexels; pp. 160–161: (border pattern) © Geordanna Cordero/Unsplash; pp. 170–171: (border pattern) © cottonbro/Pexels.

Every possible effort has been made to identify and contact all rights holders and obtain their permission for work appearing in these pages. Any errors or omissions brought to the publisher's attention will be corrected in future editions.

© 2023 Assouline Publishing
3 Park Avenue, 27th Floor
New York, NY 10016   USA
Tel: 212-989-6769   Fax: 212-647-0005
assouline.com

ISBN: 9781649800725
Printed in China.